Literature and Devotion in Later Medieval England

A selection of manuscripts from Durham University Library

— RICHARD GAMESON —

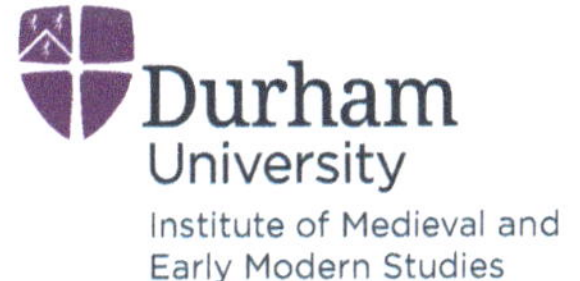

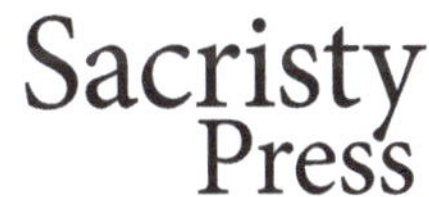

Sacristy Press
PO Box 612, Durham, DH1 9HT

www.sacristy.co.uk

First published in 2021 by Sacristy Press, Durham

Sacristy Limited, registered in England & Wales, number 7565667

British Library Cataloguing-in-Publication Data
A catalogue record for the book is available from the British Library

ISBN 978-1-78959-185-9

Cover images: Cosin V.iii.5, fol. 1r (no. 9); Cosin V.v.19 (illustration: fol. 72v); Add. 754 (illustration: p. 321).

Contents

Summum. I am the welle who so drynkith of þt water he shal nat thriste ayeyn. After this Jonathas eet of the fruyt of the second tree which restored al þt was lost þt is to seyn whan man is glorified in eternel lyf and helith the kyng þt is to seyn resoun. and so he curith the skyn of the chirche. and to his paums þt is to seyn his flessh he purueieth water of contricioun & fruyt of penance and sharpnesse for which the flessh þt is to seyn carnel or flesshly affeccioun sterueth and dieth. and the man purchaceth & getith by penitence the goodes þt weren lost. and so he gooth in to his contree þt is to seyn the regne of heuene to which god of his grace brynge vs all Amen

Ego sum fons ... bibevit &c.

Go smal book to the noble excellence
Of my lady of Westmerland and seye
Hir humble seruant with al reuerence
Him recomandith vn to hir noblesse
And byseeche hire on my behalue & preye
Thee to receyue for hir owne right
And looke thow in al manere weye
To plese hir wommanhede do thy myght

humble seruant to your gracious noblesse
T. Hoccleue

Perlegi 166[illegible]

Cosin V.iii.9, fol. 95r (no. 5)

Introduction

"To pray and rede that was evere hir lyve."

Lydgate, *Lyf of Our Lady*, I.414; **no. 3**

"For whan I had a whyle in the book red | with the speeche of Resoun was I wel fed."

Hoccleve, *Complaint*, ll. 314–15; **no. 5**

This publication presents a selection of late medieval manuscripts of English origin or provenance chosen to illustrate multiple aspects of the interlocking themes, literature and devotion. The twenty-six items offer a cross-section not only of texts, but also of physical formats, of types of decoration, and of provenance. There are works in English and in Latin, in verse and in prose, with some texts that are relatively common (e.g. **nos. 3**, **8** and **9**) and others that are rare (e.g. **nos. 11**, **13** and **17**), even unique (**no. 14**). There are manuscripts that were written by a single hand (e.g. **nos. 2–5**, **14** and **21**) and others that were the product of teams of copyists (e.g. **nos. 5**, **10**, **11**, **15**, **20** and **24**). While most of the scribes in question are (now) anonymous, a few have recorded their names in our books (**nos. 5**, **11**, **15**, **21**), one (John Heinemann) also giving his location and the precise date on which he finished the work (**no. 21**). Among the scribes who identified themselves was no less a figure than Thomas Hoccleve (**no. 5**).

This same autograph volume (**no. 5**) also highlights an important aspect of provenance, namely that our corpus includes items that were owned by women, not just by men, since the envoi to which Hoccleve appended his signature dedicated the book to Joan Beaufort, countess of Westmorland. The text in question, Hoccleve's *Series*, is a collection of secular verse by a layman. The content of the other volume that was demonstrably owned by a woman (Jane FitzLewis) was sacred verse from the pen of a monk—the *Lyf of Our Lady* by Lydgate (**no. 3**). While the original patron/dedicatee of Lydgate's *Lyf* was a man—King Henry V—that of our **no. 4** (John Walton's translation of Boethius) was a woman (Elizabeth Berkeley). Equally, two of the three texts in **no. 11** were addressed to "a religious woman".

Medieval book-owners would have had at least a general awareness of the materials used and the methods involved in manufacturing the volumes on their shelves; indeed, the processes and their rationales are occasionally mentioned in the texts themselves. Thus the act of preparing the basic material for a manuscript is alluded to in *The Privity of the Passion* (**no. 17**), where we are told that Christ was "spred on þe cross more streyt þan any parchemyn skyn is spred on þe harwe [frame]" (fol. 5v). The *Philobiblon* (**no. 7**) lists the various craftsmen involved in making a book (ch. 8, fol. 187r)—scribes (*scriptores*), correctors (*correctores*), binders (*colligatores*), and illuminators (*illuminatores*). It also echoes Cassiodorus' articulation of the spiritual benefits arising from the act of transcribing religious texts: it is "blessed exertion, laudable application to preach to men by the hand, to restore speech with the fingers, to give silent salvation to mortals, and to fight with pen and ink against the devious deceptions of the devil" (ch. 16, fol. 199r). Towards the end of *Troilus and Criseyde* (**no. 1**, fol. 104v), by contrast, Chaucer fretted that his work might be misspelled, miscopied and misunderstood: "And for þat þer is so grete diuersite | In englesh and in writing of oure tunge | So prey I god þat none miswrite þe | Ne þe mismeter for defaut of tunge | And red wherso þou bee or els sunge | þat þou be vnderstonde, god I beseche" (ll. 1793–8). Lydgate, whose work appears in **nos. 2** and **3**, articulated the impact of an effective illumination: "Of fortune turnyng the book, I fond | A meditaioun which first cam to myn hond | Tofor which was sett out in picture | Of Marie an ymage ful notable | Lyke a pyte depeynt was the figure | With weepying eyen, and cheer most lamentable | Thouh the proporcioun by crafft was agreable | Hir look doun cast with teerys al bereyned | Of hertly sorwe so soorre she was consstreyned" ("The Fifteen Joys and Sorrows of Mary", ll. 6–14). The *Philobiblon* again (ch. 17, fols. 201r–203r) sets out the appropriate way to treat books so that they will last.

A speciality of Durham University is the scientific study of medieval manuscripts. Accordingly, the pigments that were used in our volumes have been identified via the non-invasive, non-destructive techniques of

Raman spectroscopy, fibre optic reflectance spectroscopy, multispectral imaging, and X-ray fluorescence. It is hoped that publishing reliable data about the materials used in a selection of "ordinary" books (in contrast to the deluxe ones that have typically been the focus of such scientific analysis as has been accomplished to date) will be of enduring interest and value. One Durham manuscript contains, amidst a compilation of predominantly medicinal prescriptions in Middle English, a recipe for making the pigment white lead (Cosin V.iii.10, fol. 34v). It is a succinct account of a procedure familiar from multiple sources; however, as this particular version has never been published, it seems worth including it here:

> For to make whyte led and ceruse. Take a new erthen potte & put there to a good quantyte of good stronge veneg[er] & take thyn plates of led & heng them in the pot so þat it touche not the veneg[er] & stop þe pot close þat non ayre go ovte & þe myghte of the veneg[er] shal make whyte messe on the plates & scrape þat of & thys is whyte ledde. And yef it be plates of tyn it is seruse & so gader the whytnesse till al the plates be consumed & wasted.

White lead features as a pigment in **nos. 8**, **17**, **19–22** and **24–25**. In addition, it was the basis for making red lead (*minium*), which appears in **nos. 8**, **19–22** and **24–5**.

The pigments that were genuinely ubiquitous in later medieval England were vermilion and azurite, the standard materials of rubrication and text articulation. Those in regular use for illumination during Chaucer's lifetime were as follows: red—vermilion, red lead, organic; pink—organic; orange—red lead, red lead plus massicot, ochre, organic; green—copper-based (verdigris), vergaut (indigo plus orpiment); blue—azurite, lapis lazuli, mixtures of azurite and lapis lazuli; purple—organic (orchil or folium), azurite plus organic red, indigo; brown—ochre, organic; black—carbon; grey—lapis ash, carbon plus white lead; white—white lead; gold—gold leaf. Yellow was little used in the fourteenth century (see, e.g., **no. 26**); when unavoidable, it might be supplied by ochre, orpiment, realgar or organic colourants, materials that were unstable, liable to degrade other colours, fugitive or unable to supply bright, suffused hues, as the case may be (see **no. 24**). A major change in the palette that occurred immediately after Chaucer's death was the adoption of a new yellow—lead-tin yellow (Type I: lead stannate). Luminous and stable with good covering power, this pigment permitted yellow to become a more prominent element of illumination both in its own right (see **no. 9**) and in mixtures, enhancing the range of colours and coloristic effects in regular use. Thus in **nos. 20–1** it was deployed not only as a yellow but also as a component of vergaut (i.e. mixture) greens. Fifteenth-century illumination *looks* more colourful than fourteenth-century work because it *is* more colourful.

The subtlety with which pigments might be deployed even in a relatively modest manuscript may be appreciated from the historiated initial that heads our copy of Mirk's *Festial* (**no. 9**), the only decoration in the book. The blue outline of the letter is azurite, the red filling vermilion, the "white" lines between them blank parchment. The red-maroon used for the ground within the letter, as for the cloth over the pulpit, was created by blending vermilion with an organic red, the patterning on top of them being added with shell (i.e. ink) gold. Shell gold was also employed to add detailing to the pulpit, whose main bronze-gold colour was supplied by "mosaic gold" (a manufactured tin sulphide), shading being effected with carbon black. The grassy zone at the bottom of the composition was created via a covering of dilute copper green, onto which darker strokes were added in a pigment-rich version of the same paint, with yet darker lines in indigo and lighter ones of lead-tin yellow. The pink flesh of the figure was worked up from a mixture of vermilion and white lead, his dark blue robe from azurite with a modest admixture of lapis lazuli. As all the other blues are azurite alone and as this one could easily have been darkened with carbon or indigo, it seems likely that lapis—rare in English illumination of this date—was here deployed as a gesture of honour rather than to achieve a particular hue.

Our selection of manuscripts begins with overtly "literary" volumes, including a copy of Chaucer's *Troilus and Criseyde* and the autograph manuscript of Hoccleve's *Series*, and it ends with liturgical volumes (in the form of a couple of missals). In between, however, a key theme that the items illustrate is the extent to which these categories overlap and shade one into the other (**no. 2**, in which Lydgate's *Sege of Thebes* is accompanied by lives of SS. Alexis, Margaret and Mary Magdalene, epitomizes the phenomenon). And collectively, they embody the general point spelled out in some copies of the *Philobiblon* (ch. 1): "In libris mortuos quasi vivos invenio" ("In books I find the dead as if alive").

The form of the entries

Summary codicological details are provided in a headnote. The commentaries outline the content and nature of the volume (with particular attention paid to material in Middle English), report the pigments that are present (identifications are by Andrew Beeby, Louise Garner, Catherine Nicholson, and the present writer, undertaken as part of the AHRC-sponsored project, "The Pigments of British Illuminators"), and discuss the earliest evidence for provenance.

Postscriptum

The manuscripts were selected, and this catalogue compiled, for an exhibition that was due to be held in Palace Green Library, Durham, during June and July 2020, coinciding with the conference of the New Chaucer Society. Exhibition and conference had to be postponed owing to COVID-19; however, it was felt that the catalogue represented a useful resource in its own right, and hence it is now published independently.

Liber Bibliothecæ
Episcopalis Dunelm.
III. 5

The helpe and the grace of almighty god
thurgh the blissing of his blissid mo
dir Marie. be with vs at oure
begynnyng. helpe vs and spede vs eu
in our lyvyng and bryng vs to the
blis that neuer shal haue ending
Amen. By myn owne feble vndirstonding I fele wel
how it fareth bi other that ben in the same degre that
haue taken charge of sowles. and ben holde to teche
her parisshons. of all the principal festis that cometh
in the yere. shewinge to hem what that seyntes suf
fered and dide for goddis loue. So that they shulde haue
the more deuocion. and in helpe of seyntes. For ma

Cosin V.iii.5, fol. 1r (no. 9)

Catalogue

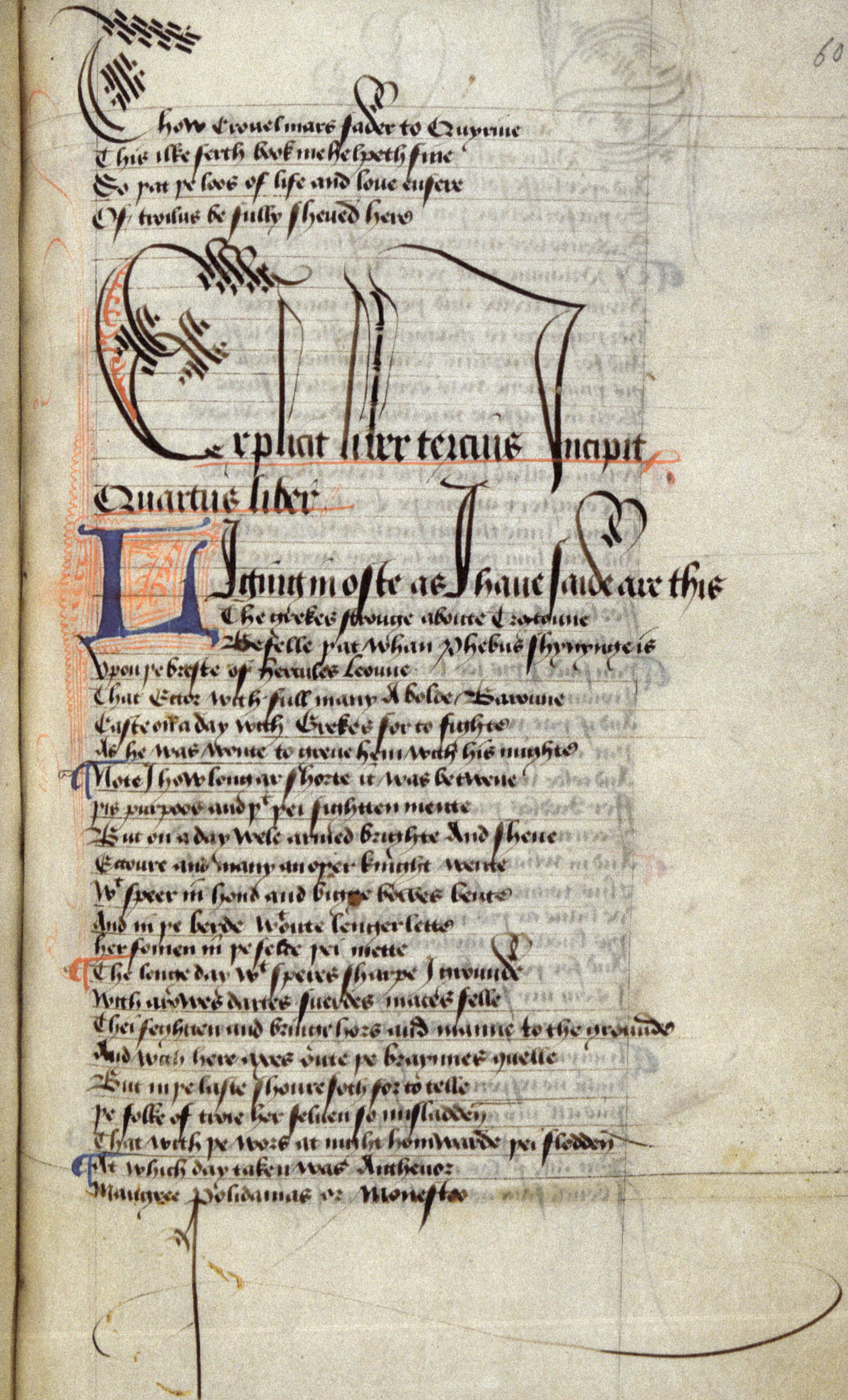

Thow crouel mars fader to Quyrine
This ilke ferth book me helpeth fine
So þat þe loos of life and loue ifere
Of troilus be fully shewed here

Explicit liber tercius Incipit
Quartus liber

Liggyng in oste as I haue saide ar this
The grekes stronge aboute Troie towne
Befelle þat whan Phebus shynynge is
Upon þe breste of Hercules Leoune
That Ector with full many a bolde Barowne
Caste on a day with Grekes for to fighte
As he was wonte to greue hem with his mighte
Not I how longe or shorte it was betwene
þis purpos and þt þei fighten mente
But on a day wele armed brighte and shene
Ectoure and many an oþer knight wente
Wt speer in hond and bigge bowes bente
And in þe berde withoute lenger lette
her fomen in þe felde þei mette
The longe day wt speres sharpe I grounde
With arowes dartes swerdes maces felle
Thei foughten and bringe hors and manne to the grounde
And with here axes oute þe braynes quelle
But in þe laste shoure soth for to telle
þe folke of troie her seluen so misladden
That with þe wors at night homwarde þei fledden
At which day taken was Anthenor
Maugree Polidamas or Monesteo

1. Geoffrey Chaucer, *Troilus and Criseyde*. England; $XV^{3/4}$

Ff. i (modern parchment) + 116 + i (modern parchment). Foliated "1"–"20", "20*"–"115". Fols. 1 and 115 are former pastedowns; fol. 114 is a part-leaf. Size: 274x165 mm (text-block: 189x96, then 190x102 mm). Lines of writing: 38–39. Ruling: ink. Quiring: 8s. Contemporary catchwords; contemporary quire letter plus leaf number on rectos in the first half of quires. Binding, *s.* xix^{med}, Charles Tuckett: brown calf over wooden boards; 6 bands; 2 metal clasps. Stains on 1r and 115v from board channels and turn-ins of an earlier structure.

Cosin V.ii.13 (illustration: fol. 60r)

The main item of the volume, *Troilus and Criseyde* (4r–105v), Chaucer's longest single poem, is here followed first by Thomas Hoccleve's *Letter of Cupid* (an English rendering of Christine de Pizan's *Epistre au Dieu d'Amour*; 106r–112v), then by a five-stanza love poem in rhyme royal, "Not long a goo purposyd I and thought | To breken of pleynly frome lusty luff[es] daunce . . . " (112v–113r), a work known only from this manuscript. That these last two items, though broadly contemporary with the Chaucer, represented a supplement is suggested by the facts that they appear on a self-contained quire and are written by a different scribe from that responsible for *Troilus*; however, their close similarities to the main book in layout and design indicate that they were designed to match it. The result is a collection that explores the travails of love from complementary perspectives: the emotional ordeals of Troilus and Criseyde before the consummation of their love, then following their enforced separation; a letter from Cupid banishing false lovers who betray and slander women; and an individual who had supposedly turned his back on love, finding himself incapable of resisting it and so begging for the favours of his lady.

In the sixteenth century, other verses with contrasting types of amatory subject matter were added informally to the front and back of the book. One hand jotted no fewer than three versions of the wistful "Whan euery woo hathe ease | And euery wysshe hys wyll | whan one thyng all men please | And euery sprying hys fyll | whan valeyes clyme the hyll | then shall my thoughtfull hart | be easyd of his smart" (2r, 115r), while another hand inserted the longer, cruder, "He bakarse boy is vere Craynke . . . My Good Boy" (running from 3r to 2v).

The text of *Troilus* transmitted here belongs to the so-called "Standard" or "Group 1" type. It was not, however, transcribed very accurately—showing to be well founded the anxiety that Chaucer articulated towards the end of the work that its words and meter might be garbled in transmission (ll. 1793–8; fol. 104v). In addition to the numerous slips that were generally corrected at an early date (fol. 69v, for example, features both omission and reduplication of words owing to eye-skip, duly rectified), the text is marred by overlooked lines and by the fact that the proem to Book IV was presented as the end of Book III (59v–60r).

An intriguing feature is the presence of two very short contributions by a second hand within a text that is otherwise entirely the work of a single scribe. As the ten lines in question (Book V, ll. 151–4 and 184–9; at the top and bottom of 83v) are not substitutions over erasures but were written on virgin parchment like the rest, it is possible that the original scribe, faced with an exemplar that was damaged, difficult to read, or obviously corrupt here (and the hypothesis of a challenging exemplar could explain other deficiencies in the transcription) had left blank spaces at these points which were filled when another source for the text of the passages became available.

The general incipit to *Troilus* is headed by a blue and red initial; subsequent books (as also the incipits of the Hoccleve and the Lover's Lament) are marked by blue initials, all flourished in red; paraphs, alternately red then blue, flag each stanza (on 97v–105v, the final quire of *Troilus*, red alone was used). The red is vermilion, the blue azurite. The first letter on each page is almost invariably enlarged and calligraphically embellished in ordinary (gallo-tannic) ink, as sometimes are other letters in the top line; on many pages one letter in the bottom line is floridly extended into the lower margin.

The earliest evidence for provenance is the *s.* xvi inscription, "Pawle keyne of London Frutrer . . . " (114v, also 1v); several slightly later jottings include the name Robert King. An inscription on 1v, which presumably related to an earlier phase in the history of the book, was erased so vigorously as to perforate the parchment and is currently illegible. The volume subsequently came into the possession of the poet William Browne (d. c. 1645), known chiefly for his *Britannia's Pastorals*; he owned five manuscripts of Middle English verse (**nos. 1–5**) that passed, via George Davenport (d. 1677), chaplain to John Cosin, bishop of Durham (d. 1672), to the library that the latter founded in Durham.

¶ Pars.

Ffirst grounde and roote of this ruyne.
As the story shal clerly determyne.
And my tale here after shal yow lere.
yf yow lyst the remenaunt for to here.

Explicit secunda pars. Sequitur tercia pars.

O Cruel Mars ful of malencolye.
And of thi kynde hote combuste ꝛ drye.
As the sperkles shewen fro so fer.
By the stremes of red ster
In thi spere as it aboute gothe
What was cause that thow were so wrothe.
With hem of Thebes thorogh whos feruent ire.
The Cytee brent and was sett afire.
As bokes olde wel reherce konne.
Of cruel hate rooted and begonne.
And engendred the story makyth mynde.
Only of blode corrupt and unkynde.
By incestyon callyd orygynal
Causyng a stryf dredful and mortal.
Of whiche the meschef thorogh al grece ran.
And kyng Adrastus alder first began.
That hath hym cast a conquest for to make.
Vpon Thebes for Polymytes sake.
In knyghtly wyse ther to preue his myght.
Of ful entent to recure his ryght.
And first of al he sent a pleynement.
And hath his lres and messegers sent.
Through oute grece to mony sondry kynges.
Hem to exhorte and make no lettynges.
And rounde aboute as made his mencyon.
He sent also to mony regyon.
Ffor princes. dukes lordes and barons.

2. John Lydgate, *Sege of Thebes*, etc. England; XV$^{3/4}$

Ff. i (*s.* xix parchment) + iii (a *s.* xvii paper leaf, within a parchment bifolium) + 113 + i (*s.* xix parchment). 294x195 (193x117) mm. Lines: 32. Ruling: ink. Quiring: 8s. Contemporary catchwords; contemporary quire letters and leaf numbers in the first half of quires (starting at "b1" owing to the loss of the first quire). Binding, *s.* xix^{med}, Tuckett: brown leather over wooden boards; 6 bands; 2 metal clasps. Stains on i recto and 113v from the turn-ins of an earlier binding.

Cosin V.ii.14 (illustration: fol. 34r)

The volume opens with the *Sege of Thebes* by John Lydgate (d. c. 1449), monk of Bury St Edmunds (fols. 1r–68v; acephalous owing to the loss of the first quire). Based on a version of the French prose *Roman de Thèbes* and enriched from Boccaccio's *Genealogiae deorum*, this is an overt continuation of Chaucer's *Canterbury Tales*, Lydgate presenting himself as a pilgrim to Canterbury who joins Chaucer's pilgrims for their return journey and, when invited to tell a tale, offers an account of Thebes from foundation to destruction. Five copies of the work are, in fact, joined to manuscripts of the *Canterbury Tales*. Here, however, it is followed by the rhyme royal version of the moralizing *Disticha Catonis* (*parvus* then *magnus*: 69r–70r, 70r–92r) from the pen of Benedict Burgh (d. 1483), an avowed admirer of Lydgate; then come a Life of St Alexis (92r–97v), Lydgate's Life of Margaret (97v–106r), and finally a Life of Mary Magdalene (106r–111v; lacking the very end owing to the loss of a leaf), all in the vernacular.

Entirely the work of a single scribe, who started each successive text on the same sheet—often the same page—as its predecessor, all presented in matching styles, the volume shows how texts of divers genres (an epic tale that could function as a mirror for princes and a plea for peace and good government, moralizing proverbs, hagiography), of different forms (the final item is prose, the rest verse), and of differing popularity (the first two texts survive in over thirty manuscripts, the others in fewer than ten) travelled together. Thus while the present manuscript and **no. 1** are physically similar, they present a striking contrast in terms of thematic coherence.

Although handsomely conceived and written in a formal script (Textualis semi-quadrata), the aesthetic effect of the book is undermined by the modest quality of the parchment and the variability of the scribe's hand. There is often a pronounced contrast in tone and texture between the hair and the flesh sides of the membrane, with numerous other imperfections. Most strikingly, the top third of fol. 2 and that of fol. 7 were reconstituted from large, neatly crafted inserts prior to writing: as the leaves are two halves of the same bifolium, it seems likely to have been flawed parchment rather than scribal error that required the reconstruction of these abutting areas. The inherent irregularities of the writing were exacerbated by variations in the parchment surface and by the scribe's poor control of pen and ink alike: he regularly dipped only after his pen had run short of ink and then overcharged it, with the result that, while some letters blot and bleed, others grow faint; corrections *in rasura* add to the visual variety. The red ink rubrics were similarly prone to bleeding and blotting.

The Cato and Book II of the Lydgate are headed by an enlarged initial in red and blue, the other major divisions by blue ones, all flourished in red. The pigments are vermilion and azurite, which were also used for paraphs and for the running headings in the Lydgate. The rubrics are written in vermilion.

The earliest evidence for provenance is a *s.* xvi^{med} inscription on fol. 8r: "James elwood of Canterbberye servant with master Railton"; the latter is likely to be the Richard Railton who was Mayor of Canterbury in 1562–3 and died in 1575.

3. John Lydgate, *Lyf of Our Lady*. England; XV$^{2/4\text{-med}}$

Ff. i (modern parchment) + 94 + i (modern parchment). 287x197 (194–216x97) mm. Lines: 35 (starting on the top ruled line). Frame-ruled in ink or lead (a frame with a lower horizontal in the first three quires, without one thereafter). Quiring: largely 8s. Leaves in the first half of quires are marked with quire letter and leaf number. Binding, xix^{med}, Tuckett: brown calf over wooden boards; 7 bands; 2 metal clasps. Traces on 1r and 94v (raised former pastedowns) from an earlier structure with 5 board channels at right angles to the spine.

Cosin V.ii.16 (illustration: fol. 5r)

Our manuscript offers one of the best texts of this lengthy verse, *Life of the Virgin Mary,* extant in some fifty copies; accordingly it served as the basis for the modern critical edition. The work begins with the note: "This booke was compileded by John Lidgate Monke of Bury. At the excitation and stirrying of our worshipfull prince, Kyng Harry the fifthe" (3r). Henry V (d. 1422) had also commissioned the French translation of the *Meditationes vitae Christi*, an account of the life and passion of Christ that was one of Lydgate's principal sources here.

The manuscript was written in a compact Secretary by a single scribe, who was also responsible for the Middle English chapter summaries (done in red and set in the margins) and for the Latin marginalia (identifying sources and expanding citations, again done in red).

The extant witnesses vary in how they structure the text, with subdivision into three, four or six books, and into thirty-six, forty-one, fifty-eight, sixty, seventy, eighty-six or eighty-seven chapters, the most common arrangement being a continuous run of eighty-seven chapters (without any book divisions), preceded by preface and chapter list. This was initially the form of the present copy, each chapter being headed by a blue initial, flourished in red, the prologue (5r) distinguished by a larger initial in both blue and red, with flourishing and border extensions in both colours (the red is vermilion, the blue azurite; for the prologue alone, indigo was deployed as well). However, in the sixteenth century its text was reorganized into four books, each with its own chapter numbering: a humanistic hand laboriously reworked the chapter numbers both in the main text and in the capitula list and substituted book for chapter numbers in the running headings. Lambeth Palace Library, MS 344 (*s.* xv^{med}) has been identified as a likely model for this reworking.

The earliest indications of provenance are martyrology entries for 21–27 April that were added in the later fifteenth century to the end of the book, seemingly starting over an erasure (90v, immediately after the end of the Lydgate) and continuing on previously blank pages (91r–92r): the only entries of a "local" nature—the Deposition of Anselm (who is described as "sancti patris nostri domini") and the feast of Mellitus, first bishop of London, third archbishop of Canterbury—hint at connections with the south-east of the country. Inscriptions added c. 1500 to fols. 1v ("Iesu Marry | thys boke ys Jane Fyz loy wys") and 94r, plus a FitzLewis armorial, indicate that by then the book belonged to Jane FitzLewis of the FitzLewis family of Bromford and Horndon, Essex.

The prolog

O thoughtfull herte plongede in high destresse
Wt slombre of slouthe this long wynters nyght
Oute of the slepe of mortall hevynesse
Awake a noon and loke upon the lyght
Of thelke sterre that wt hir bemys bryght
And withe the shynyng of hir stremys merye
Is wonte to gladde all our hemysperye
And to oppresse the derkenesse and the doole
Of hevy hertes that sorowen ad syghen ofte
I mene thylke sterre of the bryght poole
That wt hir bemys whan she is a lofte
May al the trouble aswagen and asofte
Of worldely wawes which in this mortall see
Have us byset withe grete adversitee
The rage of which is so tempestyous
That whan the calme is moste blandysshyng
Then is the streme of dethe moste perylous
If that we wante the light of hir shynyng
And but the syght allas of hir lokyng
Fro dethes brynke so make us to escape
The haven of lyfe by us may not be take
This sterre in beautee passethe pliades
Bothe of shynyng and of stremes clere
Boetes Arthour and also Iades
And Esperus when it dothe appere
For this is Spica wt hir bryght spere
That towarde even at mydnyght and at morowe
Downe frome the hevyn adawethe all our sorowe
Whose bryght bemys shynyng frome so ferre
That cloudes blake may the light nat hyde
For this of Jacob is the fayrest sterre
That under wawes never dothe declyne
Whose cours is not under the clypyke lyne
But evyrlythe of beaute may be sene
Amyddez the cerkle of our meridyne

And right thus shee bee gan with swote lette
compleynynge vpon my perturbacion
ffor cause of myschief where with I waas met
Of me shee made this lamentacion

Allas shee seide howe that this mannes mynde
Is casten doun nowe vnto depe derknes
ffor lete the clerenes of his propre kynde
Meuynge too goo too straunche derkenes
As ofte tyme as noyous besynes
With swote mesure begynneth too entrete
Whan worldly wynde with mischief & distres
Hatthe hym be raft al swote of mirthe & mete

This is the man that some tyme waas soo free
Too whom by crafte waas yovyn for too kunn
Vppe in too hevenys too bee holde and see
And too mesure thee mevyng of the sonn
Bye witt alsoo that kunnynge had see wonn
Howe that thee mone chaungeth for too procede
And what becoms thee sterris haue y wonn
And in her speerys howe dyuersly theye mede

As victor hatth he sutilly conquered
And alle this crafte that noumbre comprehendith
ffroo whens eke where these wyndys bee arered
Thee smoothe see that turneth soo & wyndeth
And whye thee sterre that is in thee este assendeth
Efte in too weste downe a geyne too lowte
And what sperit soo besyly entendith
The rounde worlde that wyndeth alle a bowte

And what attempreth soo thee lusty houres
Of that ilke fayre first somyr seeson
Araye it wt reede roose floures
Thee whiche in wynter staris bee & geson
Alle theese loo coude hee shewe soo verray reeson

4. Boethius (trans. John Walton), *Consolation of Philosophy*. England; XV²

Ff. i (modern parchment) + 113 + i (modern parchment). A paper book (fols. 2–112) with parchment endleaves (fols. 1 + its stub [1*], 113). Watermarks include forms akin to Briquet 3547 and 12436. 286x192 (202x118) mm. Lines: 33–5. Frame-ruled in ink. Quiring: mainly 12s. Contemporary catchwords; quire letter plus leaf number on leaves in the first half of quires (mainly lost through trimming). Binding, xix^{med}, Tuckett: red-brown leather over wooden boards; 6 bands; 2 metal clasps. Fol. 1r bears traces of board channels (at right angles to the spine) and turn-ins from an earlier structure.

Cosin V.ii.15 (illustration: fol. 7r)

Other copies of this English verse rendering of *De consolatione Philosophiae* by Boethius (d. c. 524) ascribe the work to John Walton, canon of Osney Abbey, Oxford, and state that it was accomplished in 1410; the first printed edition (1525) concludes with four acrostic stanzas whose initial letters name the translator (Iohannes Waltwnem) and the dedicatee (Elisabeth Berkeley). The latter is identified as the daughter of Sir Thomas fourth Lord Berkeley (d. 1417), himself an important patron of translations from Latin into Middle English prose; she married Richard Beauchamp, earl of Warwick, and died in 1422. The translation survives in more than twenty copies, suggesting that it enjoyed greater popularity than Geoffrey Chaucer's slightly earlier prose *Boece*, of which only ten copies and a paraphrase are known. Chaucer's version was, nevertheless, Walton's principal source, amplified with reference to the widely circulated commentary on *De consolatione Philosophiae* by the Dominican scholar, Nicholas Trevet (d. c. 1334).

Our copy was carelessly transcribed with two blocks of text displaced; yet this was apparently unnoticed by the single scribe. He wrote a hybrid cursive with many Secretary and some Anglicana forms, extending ascenders in the top line of the page with a rare persistence; his hand reappears in Oxford, Bodleian Library, Bodley 283, a copy of *The Mirroure of the Worlde* famous for its illustrations by the so-called Caxton Master. There is no artwork in the present book: it is articulated only by plain red initials, plus red braces of differing forms around, and a red flourish heading each stanza, all done in vermilion. Up to 16v the first letter of each line was stroked in red; a few letters were so treated between 17v and 21v, none thereafter.

The earliest evidence for the provenance of the volume takes the form of names added in various *s.* xvi hands. Several of these—including "This is Edmund Mariet booke . . . " (103v, also 56r, 91v, 98v) and "Pleasure peryshethe lightelye but honnor is immortall. Quothe J. Thornchull / Thornehull" (113r)—are casual jottings. The inscription that was added immediately below the explicit to the main text on 112v, by contrast, was arranged more formally and, although much of it has been thoroughly obliterated, the name at the end was untouched—"Harry Morely". It is possible that this refers to Henry Parker, Lord Morley (d. 1556), peer of the realm, famous for his translations from Latin and Italian, copies of which he presented to Henry VIII and Mary I.

5. Thomas Hoccleve, autograph verse and prose. London, 1421x26

Ff. i (modern parchment) + 2 (*s.* xvii paper, foliated "1"–"2") + 10 (*s.* xvi/xvii paper, foliated "3"–"12") + 83 (*s.* xv parchment, foliated "13"–"95") + i (modern parchment). 230x168 (148x104) mm. Lines: 23–4 ruled, 21 written. Ruling: brown ink (very faint). Quiring: mainly 8s. Contemporary catchwords; contemporary leaf numbering survives in some quires. Binding, *s.* xix^{med} (rebacked 2002): brown russia over wooden boards; 6 bands; 1 metal clasp.

Cosin V.iii.9 (illustration: fol. 74v)

This celebrated copy of the so-called *Series* by Thomas Hoccleve (d. 1426) was transcribed by the poet himself. It features his *Complaint* (3r–8r), *Dialogue* (9r–26v), *Jereslaus' Wife* (26v–49v), a moralization of *Jereslaus* with a prologue (49r–52v), *Lerne to Dye* (52v–74v), a lesson and homily for All Saints Day (75r–77r), and *Jonathas*, preceded by a prologue and followed by a moralization (77r–95v). Common strands linking most of these disparate works are the persona of the poet himself and the theme of how he came to compose them: *Complaint* concerns a period of malady and isolation from which Hoccleve recovered thanks to reading; *Dialogue* passes from the weary poet's labours on *Lerne to Dye* to consider his obligation to compose an appropriate collection for Duke Humphrey of Gloucester, which might also serve to remedy his unpopularity among female readers, ending with him resolving upon a story from the *Romayn Deedis*; with its long-suffering heroine, *Jereslaus' Wife*, the tale in question, could, in addition to entertaining Humphrey, pacify women who had been affronted by Hoccleve's *Letter of Cupid*; while *Jonathas*, a fable of a young man deceived by a wayward woman, would instruct the unruly son of an unnamed friend. As a set, these works invite reflection on the processes and paradoxes of reading and writing more generally.

Hoccleve supplied this copy with an envoi (95r): "Go smal book to the noble excellence | Of my lady of Westmerland and seye | hir humble seruant with al reuerence | him recommandith vn to hir nobleye | And byseeche hir on my behalue & preye | Thee to receyue for hir owne right | And looke thow in al manere weye | To plese hir wommanhede do thy might. ¶Humble seruant to your gracious nobless. T. hoccleue." He thus dedicated this volume to Joan Beaufort, countess of Westmorland (d. 1440), aunt of Duke Humphrey (and Henry V), niece of Geoffrey Chaucer.

Consonant with its status as a presentation copy, the manuscript is neatly written in a larger than usual version of Hoccleve's Secretary hand (with still larger, more formal lettering for headings), and it is elegantly articulated: the individual texts and the envoi are headed by initials of burnished gold set against panels divided into zones of blue and maroon and enhanced by foliate sprays touched with gold and green; certain subdivisions (including changes of speaker) and the Latin marginalia are flagged by paraphs of gold or blue, generally in alternation. Nevertheless, the blue that was used was the cheaper mineral azurite, not lapis lazuli, nor even a mixture of the two (a common expedient at this date).

A plethora of jotted names, pen-trials and scribbles, added in divers hands, attests to a casual attitude towards the volume during the sixteenth century (the Thomas Kyngston and Thomas Hecker who annotated 26v and 63r respectively at least claimed to have "Rede this goddly boke" and "Red all Thys boke"). This changed when it came into the possession of the antiquary John Stow (c. 1525–1605), who himself supplied the text on fols. 3–12 (replacements for *Complaint* and for *Dialogue* lines 1–252, the original versions of which had evidently been damaged or lost by that date). Thence it passed to the poet William Browne of Tavistock (see **no. 1**), before being acquired by George Davenport and donated to Cosin's library.

The other .iij. partes which in this book
Of the tretice of deeth expressed be
Touche y nat day / yt labour y forsook
ffor so greet thyng to swich a fool as me
Ouer chargeable is by my leautee
To medle wt / ynow the firste part
ffor my smal konnynge is and symple art

But as the .xe. lesson which is rad
In holy chirche / vp on an halwey day
Witnessith / syn it ioieful is and glad
ffor hem yt hens shuln wel departe away
And to the blisse go yt lastith ay
Translate wole y / nat in rym but prose
ffor so it best is / as yt y suppose

How sweet ioie and blisse is shapen to hem
yt so shuln passe hens / vp to the Citee
Callid celestial Ierusalem
After our myght and possibilitee
Let vs considere / al thogh it so be
That for to comprehende yt gladnesse
Verraily no wit may ne tonge expresse

donavit predicta tibi narrare. ut ad eterna gaudia nos-
cat pervenire.

Explicit liber de doctrina d-
di et tacendi ab albertano causid-
brixiensi de hora sancte Agathe c-
positus et compilatus sub anno domini m° cc°
quinto die mensis Dec-

Incipiunt Rubrice consolationis et consilii predicta All-

V° principit prolog. fo° 28.

6. Albertano of Brescia, Treatises. England; XIV/XV

Ff. i (modern parchment) + 173 + i (modern parchment). Two foliations: *s.* xv ink (now imperfect); *s.* xix and xx in ink then pencil (followed here). A composite volume of two parts—A) fols. 2–19; B) fols. 20–172—brought together by xv², plus medieval flyleaf (fol. 1) and *s.* xvii paper insert (fol. 1*). 176x123 mm. Binding, xix^{med}: brown russia over wooden boards; 5 bands; 1 metal clasp. Part B: text-block, 126x76 mm; 2 columns; 28 lines; ruling, lead; quiring, 8s; contemporary catchwords in scrolls, that on 59v with a face; contemporary quire letters plus leaf numbers.

Cosin V.iii.22 (illustration: fol. 34v)

The first part of this composite volume is a copy, dating from c. 1300, of the *Visio Turkilli*—an account of an Essex peasant's monitory vision of the afterlife. The substantial remainder is devoted to the three treatises of the Italian notary Albertano of Brescia (d. c. 1270): *Ars loquendi et tacendi* (20r–34v), *Liber consolationis et consilii* (34v–83r), and *De amore et dilectione Dei et proximi* (83r–172r). These are followed by verses of Peter Damian (d. 1072) that accompany works by Albertano in other manuscripts (172r–v).

All three of Albertano's texts were known to Chaucer. He drew upon *Ars loquendi et tacendi* in "The Manciple's Tale" and on *De amore et dilectione* in "The Merchant's Tale"; his most significant debt, however, was to *Liber consolationis et consilii.* This work (dated in its explicit to April and May 1246) explored via dialogue between the husband and wife, Melibeus and Prudence, the appropriate response to a violent assault on the latter and their daughter, the husband's hot-headed wish for revenge being replaced with reconciliation thanks to the counsels of his wife—prudent both in name and nature. Exceptionally popular, the work was translated into various European vernaculars, *Mélibée et Prudence*, the French rendering of 1337 by the Dominican Renaut de Louhans being the immediate source of Chaucer's "Tale of Melibee", the one complete tale that the poet presents as told by himself.

The present copy of Albertano's works was written by a single scribe in Anglicana formata, with Textualis semi-quadrata for display script; its functional section initials were done in azurite, flourished with vermilion. Liberally annotated and carefully corrected by several contemporaries writing varieties of Secretary ("cor" for "correctus" or "corrigitur" was discreetly added to the bottom of many pages), the manuscript underlines the availability in Chaucer's England of Albertano's writings in their original form and highlights the attention that they received here from early readers.

7. Richard de Bury, *Philobiblon*. England or France; XV^{med}

Ff. i (paper) + 2 (medieval leaves recycled as flyleaves, foliated "i", "ii") + 208 + 2 (medieval leaves recycled as flyleaves, foliated "209", "210") + i (paper). 172x112 (108x69—written above top line) mm. Lines: 28–30. Ruling: ink. Quiring: generally 12s (some with losses); 8s for part of the *Philobiblon*. Quire letter plus leaf number in the first half of quires. Binding, *s.* xvii (?Hutchinson of Durham), rebacked *s.* xix^{med}: millboard boards covered in sprinkled brown leather, outlined with a double blind fillet, a further double blind fillet parallel to the spine; edges rolled with a broken golden line; 4 bands; 1 metal clasp. Traces on i recto and 210v from the turn-ins of an earlier binding; holes in i and rust stains on ii from the fixtures for a pair of metal clasps.

Cosin V.v.2 (illustration: fol. 193v)

The *Philobiblon* (161r–208r) is preceded by copies of Alan of Lille's *Anticlaudianus* (1r–78v, the incipit lost) and *De planctu naturae* (80r–124v), then Geoffrey of Vinsauf's *Poetria nova* (125r–160r). The work of each author appears on its own set of quires wholly or partly written by its own scribe; however, parity of format, the reappearance of the Alan of Lille scribe for the last four quires of the *Philobiblon*, and a continuous series of early quire letters leave no doubt that the three parts were designed to go together. Each surviving incipit is headed by a blue initial, flourished in red, subdivisions being marked by plain blue initials (on fols. 1r–24r and 171v, further articulation was supplied in red). The blue is azurite, the red vermilion.

If the hands of the three original scribes (varieties of Secretary) would be as much at home in France as in England, an early English provenance is suggested by the nature of the hands responsible for the list of contents on ii verso and for three short *s.* xv^{2} additions on 78v–79r. The earliest evidence of specific ownership is the inscription that was added to the top of ii verso, c. 1500: "Pertinet R Langley" (possible candidates of the right period include the Ralph Langley who was a monk of Westminster from 1465/6–1501, and the man of the same name who studied canon law at Cambridge in 1488 and is recorded as vicar at Prestwich, Lancashire, in 1493).

The preface to the *Philobiblon* begins with a salutation from Richard de Bury, bishop of Durham 1333–45, and the final chapter ends with a colophon attributing the text to him and (in some cases, though not here) stating that it was completed at his manor of Bishop Auckland, Co. Durham, in January 1344; however, certain copies also incorporate a note naming the Dominican Robert Holcot (d. 1349) as its editor. How much of the work was due to Richard as opposed to Robert is accordingly a matter of debate.

The page reproduced (193v) shows the beginning of Chapter 13, a defence of *fabulas poetarum* ("the fables of the poets"). The works in question are those of classical antiquity; however, some of the points—that such literature can be an enticing and accessible way to convey knowledge and moral values—could equally be applied to secular English verse. Here, as elsewhere in the text, this scribe has left occasional gaps—presumably because he could not read the words in his exemplar at these points or recognized them as faulty (the space at Chapter 13, line 4, for example, should contain "obscena", while the list of book professionals in Chapter 8 that was mentioned in the Introduction has a gap where the word "antiquariorum" should appear).

graphiam prosodiam ethimologiam ac diasin
tesim inconcusse curiositate consideravimus. Ter-
minos vetustate nimia caligantes destru-
sionibus congruis delucidare curavimus, et fe-
cimus ne planam viris studentibus pateremus.
Hoc est sane summa totalis quare tot gramma-
ticorum antiquata volumina emendatis co-
dicibus studuimus ut semitas regias sternere-
mus quibus ad artes quaestuosas in futurum
scolares incederent inoffense.

Quare non omnino necleximus fabulas poetarum.

Omnia genera machinarum quibus contra
poetas solent inde vitiatis amato-
res obicere duplici refellimur
Quoniam ipsa vel in   materia gratis
cultoris sui animus adiscet vel quod ficta sub ho-
nesta tractatur sive naturalis vel historia-
lis veritas indagatur sub eloquiis typice fic-
tionis ipsius nimirum omnes homines natu-
raliter scire desiderent nec tamen omnes equa-
liter delectantur insistere ipsius studii labo-
re gustato et sensuum fatigacione percepta
plerique mentem abiciunt inconsulta pru-
insipienter testa solita melioris attingentur.
Similiter est enim homini duplex amor videlicet de
libertatis in regie et aliquantulum voluptates in
opere. Unde nullus sine causa alieno se
subdit imperio vel operis quicquam exercet
cum tedio sua sponte. Delicias namque

preieris / And also lord ȝeue þou
to me in myldenesse to be mesu
rid in word. þat y gete silence:
and þat y speke þat þing þat
bisemeþ. & þat y holde stille þat
þing þat bisemeþ not to speke
ȝeue me grace to kepe þe feiþ un
wemmyd. wiþouten ony errour:
and my werkis to be worþi up
feiþ / Al þis sentence seiþ seynt
austyn: in his book to þe eerl

Of goostli bataile.

Almyȝti god god seiþ bi
hooli iob. þat al mannes
lyf upon erþe is fiȝtyng: þat is
aȝens goostli enemyes & synne

8. Pore Caitif. England; $XV^{1/4}$

Ff. ii (*s.* xx paper) + i (*s.* xvii parchment) + 233 + i (*s.* xvii parchment) + ii (*s.* xx paper). Ink pagination (erased ink foliation). 105x74 (70x49) mm. Lines: 16. Ruling: ink. Quiring: 8s (a quire lost after p. 128). Contemporary catchwords. Binding: *s.* xx (1930x86): brown morocco; 3 bands.

Add. 754 (illustration: p. 321)

The purpose of this collection of fourteen tracts on spiritual life, compiled by a *pore caitif* ("poor wretch"), is declared at the beginning of the prologue: it was to "teche symple men and wommen of good wille þe rigt weie to heuene". The first three tracts, extended expositions of the Creed, the Ten Commandments, and the Pater noster, amount collectively to more than half of the total text (pp. 4–272 in our copy). The subsequent, shorter tracts focus on particular spiritual or devotional issues, such as "Of uerii mekenes", "Of mannes will", and "Of actiif liif and contemplative" (Tracts 11–13 respectively). Tract 8, "Of goostli batail" (pp. 321–52), reproduced here, treats the struggle of the soul against temptation (" . . . al mannes lyf upon erþe is figtyng, þat is agens goostli enemyes & synne . . . "), enlivened by an extended analogy with the accoutrements of the contemporary knight: horse, bridle and reins, saddle, and spurs are allegorized in terms of virtues. The final (longer) tract, "þe myrour off chaastite", treats bodily and spiritual purity.

The popularity of the work is attested by thirty manuscripts of the full text, plus a further twenty with extracts from it. Copies were typically produced to a compact format. Our manuscript, which is very small yet neatly and clearly written, was particularly well suited to the role of a *vade mecum*.

Decorated initials plus all-round frames head the Prologue, and tracts 1–3, 8, 11, 13 and 14. Tracts 4–7, 9, 10 and 12, by contrast, are marked more modestly by golden initials set against a pink ground within a blue panel (or vice versa) plus extension sprays. The pigments are red lead with massicot, often combined with an organic red (the resulting colour generally now degraded to brown), an organic pink, copper green, lapis lazuli blue, white lead, and a rather impure gold; vermilion was used for the rubrics and running headings and an organic purple in the flourishing, but neither features in the principal decoration.

The earliest indication of provenance is an informal jotting added to p. 269, *s.* xvi: the initial name has unfortunately been entirely cropped away, leaving only, "//From mr John turner dwelling in flytestryt". Part of the Bibliotheca Swaniana (i.e. of David Swan) in 1792, the volume subsequently belonged to the great manuscript collector Henry Yates Thompson (1838–1928), who gave it to the Cambridge historian G. M. Trevelyan (1876–1962); Trevelyan was Chancellor of Durham University from 1950–57, and his daughter, Mary Moorman (1905–94), biographer of Wordsworth, presented it to Durham University Library in 1986.

9. John Mirk, *Festial*. England; XV^{med}

Ff. i (modern parchment) + 1 (medieval flyleaf) + 165 + 1 (paper, *s.* xvi) + 2 (medieval flyleaves) + i (modern parchment). 261x196 (180–198x108–112) mm. Lines: 31–34 (written above top line). Frame-ruled in hardpoint and ink (the first two and last two horizontals extended). Quiring: 8s. The inner- and the outermost sheets of each quire are parchment, the two interior sheets paper (watermark: cf. Briquet 8941). Contemporary catchwords in scrolls. Binding, xix^{med}: brown calf over wooden boards; 6 bands; 2 metal clasps. Stains on 163v from the turn-ins of an earlier binding; green-stained hole at the centre of 163 from the pin of an earlier clasp; green stains towards the bottom of the leaf from the fixtures for a chain staple.

Cosin V.iii.5 (illustration: fol. 1r)

This sermon collection, drawn up in the late fourteenth century by John Mirk, canon then prior of Lilleshall Abbey, Shropshire, was designed to provide parish priests with homilies for the main feasts of the year. Accordingly, in his prologue Mirk asked that the work "be called *Festiall*". He further explained that it was produced as a resource for clergy who lacked books and learning, that much of the content was taken from the *Legenda Aurea* ("The Golden Legend"), and that the ultimate aim was to inculcate devotion to the saints among parishioners.

The present manuscript belongs to the so-called B group, in which the texts were reorganized into temporale (here fols. 1r–52r) and sanctorale (52r–156r), ending with a homily for the dedication of a church. It is, however, the only one of the group to be prefaced by a prayer ("The helpe and the grace of almighty god thurgh the blissing of his blissid modir Marie be with us at oure begynyng . . . ") and the prologue ("Bi myn owne feble undirstonding . . . "), both on 1r, elements otherwise restricted to group A manuscripts.

Our volume is the most handsome of the twenty or so copies of the collection as a whole. Neatly written in a single Secretary hand, it has the unique distinction of being headed by an historiated initial. This shows a cleric within a multangular pulpit, his hands pressed together, presumably in prayer. The artwork has been tentatively attributed to an illuminator who also worked on the fine Lydgate, British Library, Royal 18 D.iii. The pigments used to paint the image are: red—vermilion, and vermilion enriched with an organic red; yellow—lead-tin yellow; green—copper (two intensities) and indigo; blue—azurite, and azurite enriched with lapis lazuli; purple—organic; black—carbon and indigo; white—white lead; gold—shell (ink) gold and mosaic gold (a manufactured tin sulphide). See the Introduction for further comment. Each sermon is headed by an initial done in azurite; rubrics and other highlighted text (Latin incipits and key names) are in vermilion, as are the pen-strokes applied to some capitals; paraphs and the flourished border on fol. 1 are in azurite and vermilion.

Among the many early jottings and pen-trials on the endleaves are some verses in Middle English: "Lady of love ye will me lese | . . . | If ye be false evell may ye spede", and "I had my mony and my frend | as many a man hathe in londe | I lent my mony to my frend | as dothe bothe fre and bonde", the first copied twice by different hands (both on 162v), the second written multiple times on 162v and 163r.

The earliest evidence for provenance takes the form of various scribbled names dating from the early sixteenth century (Antony Smythe, 124r; Thomas Northe, 142v, 154r, 161v; and Wyllyam northe cetesyne of london and of cawntiberye, 157r). There are hints that the volume may have been in a printer-stationer's shop around this time: fols. 71r and 72r bear inked letter impressions from type of a sort that was used in Paris, the Low Countries and London during the first half of the sixteenth century; while jottings on 161r include "mastore Hering item fore iij skyns of parchment—vi d", "mastere garite Item fore a skyn of parchmente—ij d | Item fore paper—ij d | item fore wax—iijj d". By 1644 at the latest, the volume was in the collection of John Cosin, future bishop of Durham (1660–72): it is the only medieval manuscript listed among the books that from 1644 to 1660 he left at Peterhouse, Cambridge.

The helpe and the grace of almighty god
thurgh the blissing of his blissid mo
dir Marie. be with us at oure
begynnyng. helpe us and spede us e
in our lyvyng and bring us to the
blis that never shal haue ending
Amen. By myn owne feble understonding I fele wel
how it fareth bi othir that ben in the same degre that
haue taken charge of sowles. and ben holde to teche
her parisshons. of all the principal festis that cometh
in the yere. shewinge to hem what that seyntes suf
fered and dide for goddis love. So that they shulde haue
the more devocion. and in helpe of Seyntes. For ma
ny excusyd hem selfe bi defaute of bokes. and also by
symplenesse of kunnyng. Therfore in helpe of suche
men clerkis haue drawen out of legenda aurea. with
more addinge to this tretice folowyng. Who so that
hath lust to studie therynne. he shal fynde redy of all
the principall festes of the yere. eche on a short sermon
nedefull for hym to teche & other to lerne. And for this
tretise spekith of all high festis: therfor I wille and pray that
it be called Festiall. the which begynneth at the first Son
day of Advent in the worship of god. and all the Seyntes
that ben writen therynne.

Gode men and women ye shal knowe well. that
this day is callid the sonday of cristes comynge
which for holy churche makith mencion of the
first comyng of crist goddis sonne of heven. into this world
for to bringe mankinde out of the feendis bondage and
to bring good lyvers in to endles blisse. And his secund com
ing shalbe at the day of dome for to deme & iuge all
wrecched lyvers. unto everlasting payne. But for ye first

then in heuyn yo[ur] eu[er]lastyng rewarde and mede shalbe./ And this
is the cause it is to suppose that she beryth the palme and
sygne of a chirche in tokynynge that she of all her enmyes
hade the victory. and was the veray trewe soldier of criste
and his chirche and a shilde was./ Thus than is declared
howe this glorio[us] virgyne and martir seynt Barbara by
manyfolde tribulacions and p[er]secucions. torme[n]tes paynes and
martirdome. as a meke lambe folowede criste the veray lombe
that taketh a way o[ur] synnes and wassheth us dayly in the
blode of his blessed and glorio[us] passion. Wherfore nowe she
foloweth hym in the mery paradise of blisse berynge the crowne
of glorye upon her hede. be sette w[ith] the fresshe florysshynge
rosys and lylies on eu[er]y side of ioye and gladenes. dawnsyng
a monge the virgynall felisship of hevenly virgyns with owte
cessyng and werynesse. syngynge and sayinge w[ith] angels and
seyntes the newe songe of p[re]ysynge to the holy trinite. laus
tibi d[omi]ne rex eterne glorie. To this blissed virgyne therfore
and martir lette us pray. that she will pray for us to o[ur] lorde
ihu criste kynge of blisse that we may be his folowers worthily
clensed frome all man[er] of synne. and neu[er] to be vngette to
other but to hym and for hym whom he soo dere hath bought
with his p[re]cio[us] blode. for to make us parteners of his glory
a monge all angels and seyntes. Qui cum patre et sp[irit]u s[an]c[t]o
viuit et regnat deus in secula seculor[um] Amen.

Here endyth the lyfe and martyrdome w[ith] the translacions and invencion of the glorio[us] spouse of criste seynt Barbara. And after here foloweth the myracles of the same glorio[us] virgyne

10. *The Lyfe and Martirdome of Seynt Barbara.* England; XV^{med}

Ff. i (paper) + ii (parchment) + 77 + ii (medieval parchment leaves, recycled as endleaves) + i (paper). 200x145 mm (written area of fols. 1–48, 160x103 mm; of fols. 49–77, 151x112 mm). Lines: fols. 1–48, 24–26; fols. 49–77, 26–28. Frame-ruled in lead (fols. 1r–49r) then ink (49v–76r). Quiring: 8s; contemporary signatures. Binding, *s.* xvii, Hugh Hutchinson of Durham: millboard covered in sprinkled brown calf, outlined on three sides with a double blind fillet, a blind roll along the hinge, a further double blind fillet parallel to the spine; Hutchinson's roll G, gilt, on the edges; 4 narrow bands; 1 metal clasp; front board detached. Stain on 79v from the (generous) turn-ins of an earlier binding.

Cosin V.iv.4 (illustration: fol. 54v)

This lengthy vernacular *Lyfe and martirdome with the translacions and Inuencion of the glorious Spouse of criste Seynt Barbara*, as it is styled in its explicit (1r–54v), is based on the Latin *Vita* by the Brabantine Augustinian, Jan van Wakkerzeel (fl. xiv$^{4/4}$); the twenty-three miracles that follow (55r–76r) derive from the same source. The English Life has its own preface which begins by invoking Christ, Mary, Brigit, Augustine and "all the seintis of heven", the references to Brigit (of Sweden) and Augustine hinting at an association with the Brigittine community of Syon Abbey, well known for its literary activities. The text only otherwise occurs in the version of the *Gilte Legende* found in Lambeth Palace Library, MS 72, and in a single print extant solely as a fragment (Bodleian Library, Douce frag. e.47). The explicit to the miracles is followed by a four-line verse prayer known only from our manuscript: "Now Barbara the Spouse of criste that moche art of myght | For the loue of thi Spouse that loved the of right | Saue vs ffrom alle soden chaunces be day and be nyght | So that after this wreched lyfe we may come to endles li[ght—lost] Amen". Like the suffrages in *horae* (see **nos. 20–22**), this succinctly articulates the philosophy underlying the cult of saints: a brief acclamation of Barbara and her Christian virtue (virginity) is followed by a request for her aid first in the present life, then to smooth the suppliant's passage to heaven.

The manuscript is the work of two scribes, one responsible for the first six quires (1r–48v), the other for the remaining four (49r–77v); the differences in text-block and line count between the two stints—which also differ in ruling medium—suggest that each designed his own *mise-en-page* without reference to the other. Both write fine Anglicana hands, the first larger and more florid than the second; each accomplished his own rubrics (which the first failed to provide for Chapters 2 and 9). The same red (vermilion) was employed for stroking sentence capitals and for underlining names (the second scribe preferred not to treat "Barbara" thus) as well as words in Latin. In his first three quires (but not thereafter), the first scribe also accentuated his punctuation with it, in the first quire alone drawing a paraph-like mark over the multiple dots and dashes that signalled the ends of sentences. Azurite blue initials flourished in vermilion were supplied for the preface and incipit of the Life; the spaces reserved for coloured initials heading subsequent chapters both in the Life and in the Miracles remained unfilled.

There is no evidence for the provenance of the manuscript prior to its acquisition by George Davenport (see **no. 1**). One would dearly like to know where and when it acquired its medieval endleaves, the second of which is a fragment from a *s.* xv^{2} copy of the *Liber de distinccione metrorum* of Jacobus Nicholai of Denmark (d. after 1379). Completed in 1363, this exposition of verse forms exemplified by thirty-two *metra* about death, was dedicated to the author's patron, the countess of Pembroke, Marie de Saint-Pol, founder of Pembroke College, Cambridge, and it included as a coda a *planctus* (partly preserved here) for her long-dead husband, the earl of Pembroke, Aymer de Valence (d. 1324).

11. *Doctrine of the Hert*; *The Tree*; *XII Fruits of the Holy Ghost*. England; XV^{med}

Ff. i (modern parchment) + 2 (medieval parchment flyleaves) + 150 + 1 (medieval parchment endleaf) + i (modern parchment). Composed of three separate sections: (a) Qq. I–V (fols. 1–71); (b) VI–VII (72–91); and (c) VIII–XII (92–150). 217x150 mm. Predominantly paper (watermarks cf. Briquet nos. 23–5, 2825, 11851–94), with parchment used for the outermost bifolium of Qq. IV–V and VIII–XII, for the outer two bifolia of Q. VII, for the outermost and innermost bifolia of Qq. I–III, and throughout Q. VI. Text-block and line count vary by section and also within sections: (a) c. 164x98 mm, generally around 34 lines; (b) c. 131x90 mm, around 25 lines; (c) c. 146x105 mm, around 29 lines. Ruling: (a) and (c) frame-ruled in ink; (b) full grid in ink to 84r and on 91v, frame-ruled on 84v–91r. Quiring: variable, predominantly 14s and 16s. Contemporary catchwords in sections (a) and (b), quire letters ("a"–"e") plus leaf number on leaves in the first half of quires in (c). A continuous set of quire signatures (Roman numerals) added throughout, *s.* xv^{med-2}. Binding, *s.* xix^{med}: brown russia over wooden boards; 5 bands; 1 metal clasp.

Cosin V.iii.24 (illustration: fol. 124v)

Though made as separate, non-matching sections, the three parts of this book have a scribal hand in common and were evidently brought together at an early date (as the added, continuous quire numeration shows) to form an extended manual of spiritual instruction aimed at religious women. The same three works appear together in Cambridge, Fitzwilliam Museum, McClean 132, a unified volume copied by a single scribe.

The first text (1r–69v) is an adaptation in English for "symple soules" of the thirteenth-century *De doctrina cordis* / *De preparatione cordis* that has been associated with the Dominican Hugh of Saint-Cher or alternatively the Cistercian Gerard of Liège. Whereas there are more than 200 copies of the Latin text, the Middle English version survives in only four manuscripts including the present one. Each of the seven sections offers prescriptions for, and meditations on, an action of the "heart" (soul) facilitated by one of the seven gifts of the Holy Spirit: thus the third is "How and in what wise a mynche [monastic] shuld opyn here hert to God be þe gifte of kunnyng". The second text (72r–91v), *The Tree*, expounds spiritual growth in terms of a tree which should first "be roted in very meeknesse, to be moysted & watred in very compunction, to be extendyd and spred abrode be very charyte & at þe laste to be reysyd upon hegh be very deuocyon, þat sum tyme aftyr þys lyfe þu may be rekenyd endelesly, amonge þe holy trees of hys heuenly paradyse" (fol. 91v). Its initial rubric describes it as "a lettre of relygyous gouernaunce sent to a relygyous woman"; the author subsequently recommends reading other "deuoute bokes" "on haly days", singling out the *Stimulus amoris* (see **no. 17**) for this purpose. The third text (92r–150v), the *XII frutes of the holy goost*, is the pendant to *The Tree* and is similarly styled "a lettere sent to a relygyous woman". It considers in turn twelve fruits (spiritual virtues), beginning with "charyte" and ending with "chastyte", for each of which a sequence of virtues is enumerated. *The Tree* and *Twelve Fruits* are both known from three manuscripts including the present one.

The individual parts of the collection were written by three scribes, with interventions and corrections throughout by a further hand. The first text (1r–69v, on quires I–V) was largely the work of two scribes (responsible for 1r–43v, and 44r–69v respectively) with short interventions by a third (17r–v, 32r–v, plus passages on 30r, 39r, and 43v; his lines on this last page were subsequently deleted as they duplicated the start of scribe two's stint on 44r). The second text (quires VI–VII, fols. 72r–91v), was entirely penned by a fourth scribe, who names himself in a formulaic colophon (91v): "Nunc finem fixi penitet me si male scripsi [Baile Robertus—erased] in celum sit benedictus. Amen" ("Now I have set down the end. It grieves me if I have written badly. May Robert Baile be blessed in heaven. Amen"). Scribe three nevertheless appears here too—in the role of corrector. The third text (quires VIII–XII, fols. 92r–150v) was written by scribe two (92r–140v, 142r–150v) who on this occasion gives his name in a note filling a blank space at the end of chapter vi (124v): "Wyth mercy and pyte | Prey for þe wryhtere of thys dyhte William". His work here was corrected by scribe three, who added a supply leaf (141) to make good a substantial omission. This third hand (the corrector), though unnamed, probably

vndyrstonde correccyon and blame of thy souereyn for
thyn defawtys and by thys manna whych ys swete
yu schalt vndyrstonde swetnesse of good thyngys yt cun
nyth ye rodde of correccyon to be born paciently. wha
ne thou sufferyst yt grucchyngly. yu haste not zyt
thys manna of swete thyngys. kepe wel yn thyn arke
of god yt ys yn thyn herte. whych ys callyd goddys
howse or goddys arke mekenesse. and thanne schalt thou
fynde grete swetnesse yn correccyon of relygyon whych
rewardyth awey so thy synnys yt yu schalt at ye laste apper
afore thy spouse Jhu. wyth oute ony spot. The fourte ver
tu ys yt yt makyth ye to speke swetly and goodly of
vertu. for to multyplye many swete soulys to god.
as salomon seyth Cor dulcis est alloquio maiora repe
riet. he yt ys swete yn spekyng he seyth schal wynne ma
ny soulys to god and at the laste for hys wynnyng
schal receyue grete rewardys so a prechour among
and a souereyne yn exhortyng of hys subiectys. schulde
swetly schewe here exhortacyon and so schulde they mul
typlye the frendys of god. as salomon seyth yn an other
place Verbum dulce multiplicat amicos. A swete exhorta
cyon or prechyng multyplyth frendys to god. he seyth.
Thus to ete Systr of thys swete fruit. yt thou mowe ther by
drawe to heuene ward. and also to multyplye many
louerys owre lord the. Amen.

Wyth mercy and pyte
Prey for ye wryter of thys dyte
Wilm

reappears in Cambridge University Library, Hh.1.11, fols. 45r–53v, 55r–60r (respectively a dialogue about the sacrament and a meditation on Mary, both in the vernacular). Scribe one regularly extended strokes into the margins, embellishing them with spirited but artistically mediocre calligraphic flourishes. The volume has no other ornamentation, and the spaces reserved for initials remain unfilled.

One copy of *Doctrine of the Heart* is recorded in a documentary source dated 1481—the will of Margaret Purdans of Norwich, long-time widow of a former mayor of that city. This reveals that the testator had given or lent a copy of *Le doctrine of the herte* to Margaret Yaxley, a nun of Bruisyard, Suffolk, a community of Poor Clares, to which house it was to pass when the latter died. There are intriguing parallels between Margaret's copy and our manuscript. In addition to its East Anglian dialect and orthography, our volume bears on two flyleaves the name "Welles" (ii recto and 151v—in the former case associated with a verse: "O Jesu ful of myght markyd in þi mageste | Save our kyng bothe day and nyght | In every place wher so he be | Quod Welles"), and another beneficiary of Margaret's will was John Wellys (d. 1495), Alderman and Mayor of Norwich.

12. *Speculum Christianorum*. England; XV^{med}

Ff. iv + 206 + iii. 88x55 (59x40) mm. Lines: 17–18. Ruling: ink. Quiring: varied (8s, 12s, and a 10). Contemporary catchwords; contemporary quire letter and leaf numbering in the first half of quires starting in Q. II (Qq. I–II have contemporary numbering "1"–"2"). Binding, *s*. xv^{med}: slightly bevelled wooden boards covered in leather (still pink on the turn-ins); sewn on three double bands; head and tail reinforced with later green and yellow twine; one later metal clasp formed from two interlaced loops (there is a hole in the centre of the backboard from the pin fixture of an earlier strap-and-pin fastening); pastedowns and flyleaves from a *s*. xv service-book with lections for St Chrisogonus.

Ushaw 28 (illustration: fol. 35r)

The popularity of this manual of pastoral care in fifteenth-century England is demonstrated by the survival of nearly sixty manuscripts plus the production of three printed editions before 1501. Our copy is distinguished by the fact that it preserves its first binding, showing a "pocketbook" in its original form; the weathered and stained condition of the leaves suggests that it was extensively used. The purpose and primary audience of the work is declared in its initial rubric (found in only one other copy, Dublin, Trinity College, 351): *Incipit speculum christianorum tractatum de vno magistro apud oxoniam pro curatis* ("Here begins Mirror of Christians, a treatise from a master at Oxford for curates"). Its eight sections ("tabulae") run through the fundamentals of the faith—the Creeds, the Ten Commandments, the Seven Corporal and Seven Spiritual Works of Mercy, the Seven Virtues and Vices—before treating such topics as impediments and aids to spiritual growth, heaven and hell, along with the story of the four philosophers and their attempts to explain misfortune, the nature of the present world (sinful and transient), plus prayers to Christ and the Virgin (including *Gaude flore virginali*, a widely diffused hymn celebrating the celestial joys of Mary that was sometimes attributed to Thomas Becket).

Although primarily in Latin, the text includes sections in Middle English prose and verse (our manuscript includes an extra set of verses for the Ten Commandments that is only included in one other copy, Cambridge, Sidney Sussex College, 55). The first vernacular prose to appear comprises translations and explanations of phrases from the Pater noster (16r–17v). The last set of verses is an appeal to the Virgin Mary (105v–107r): "*Oracio ad sanctam mariam uirginem*. Mary modir Wel þow be; mary meyden þinke on me . . . And sheld me out of deedly syn; þat i neuer be takyn þer in". In common with many such prayers, it begs her to defend the suppliant from sin in all its forms, from the Devil and from Hell, and asks her to help him keep the Christian faith; it also requests help with the necessities of life, and implores that not only friends but also enemies may avoid dying in mortal sin; in accordance with the aims of the manual as a whole, it asserts that the suppliant will rehearse the Pater noster and the Creed.

In the present manuscript, the *Speculum christianorum* (4r–157v) is followed by tracts on the responsibilities of priests (157v–172v), by an anonymous *Speculum peccatoris* variously associated in different manuscripts with St Bernard, Augustine, or Richard Rolle (172v–190r), and by a tract on how to die a good Christian death (190r–208v) that is derived from the *Horologium sapientiae* of Henry Suso (d. 1366). All these texts are entirely in Latin. A final leaf, now lacking, evidently began with widely current verses on transubstantiation, only the first line of which ("Constat in altari carnem de pane creari") survives.

Notwithstanding the diminutive size and economical conception of the book, the text itself was neatly written in a relatively formal Textualis semi-quadrata. That at least the first two quires were carefully proofread is suggested by the fact that the scribe wrote the individual syllables, "cor", "ri", "gi", "tur" ("it is corrected"), in sequence over and over again, at the foot of every page therein. The main divisions and subsections are marked by enlarged initials adorned with foliate forms, plus border sprays, lightly washed in green and yellow, with occasional touches in red. The red used here and throughout is vermilion; the green is a mixture of a copper-based colorant and an organic one; the yellow is organic; the blue that was occasionally used for other initials is azurite.

dei et mandatis illius marie assiduus
esto. Ambrosius. Qui in cordibus suis dona
non habent precepta verba diuina tolle
rabunt tantum. idem. Grauissime fratres
qui ignorans. gregorius. quale se venti
putat qui regulam summe fortitudinis
ignorat. Ieronimus. absque notitia cre
atoris sui homo pecus est. Septimum
est eius vel xii. deum time et mandata
eius obserua. hoc est omnis homo glo
ad hoc est omnis homo creatus.

In heuen sijl duelle al citen
wen pat kuone te kze gode
beddinges terme

Decem dicuntur man
data dei quorum tria
pertinent ad deum
septem vero ad proximum

7 The Be hath þre kyndes. One is þt he is neuer ydel nor he is not with hem þt wil not worken but he castith hem out & puttith hem away. An other kynde of þe bee. is þis. þat when he flieth he takiþ erþe in his feete. þt he be not lyghtly heighed in the ayer with þe wynd. The thridde kynde is. þat he kepith clene his wyngys. þus on þe same wise Ryghtwisemen þt louen god ar neuer in ydelnesse. ffor eyþer þey arn in trauayle prayyng or redyng or thynkyng or sum good deed doyng. Or with undertakyng ydel men & shewyng hem worthy to ben putt fro þe rest off heuene. for þei wil not trauaylen here. Also Ryghtwisemen taken erthe in her feet. þt is to say þei holden hem self foule and erthly in her affection þt þei be not blowen away with þe wynde of vanite. and of blowyng of pride. The thridde kynd is þey kepyn her wyngys clene. þt is to say þe two comandementis of charite þei fulfillen in good consciens and þey han oþer vertues vnblemyd. with filthe of synne. & vnclene loue. And aristotle saith þt bees fighten agaynst hem þt wil drawe her hony fro hem. So shold we do agaynst fendis þt strengthen hem to reue fro us þe swete hony of clene lyff & goostly grace. ffor many arn þt neuer kunne hold þe order of loue anempte her frendis sibbe or kynnesmen. But eyþer þei louen hem ouer mekel settyng alle her thought vnskilfully on hem or þei loue hem ouer litel. yff þei don not as þei woldyn þt þei diden to hem. Suche men kunne nought fight for her hony for þe fend turnen hit to wormode & maken hem to weyghe here often tymys. and maken to hem ful bitter in angre & tene & wiþ bisines of vayn thoughtis & oþer wrecchidnesses. ffor þey arn so heuyed in erthly frendship þat þei wolden not flee in to þe loue of ihu criste. The whilke þei wil not fortoo for þe loue of al creaturs leuyng in erth. Wherfor Aristotle saith þat sum foulis arn of good flyght þt passen fro o land to an oþer. Som ar of euyl fleyng for heuynes of body & her neste is not fer fro the erthe & her liff is off þe erþe. Ryght so hit is of hem þt han turned hem to goddis seruyse. Som ar of good fleyng. for þei fleen fro þe erþe vn to heuen & resten hem þer in þought & arn fed in delitis of goddis loue & han no þought of þe los of þe worlde. Som ar þt now kon flee fro þe lond but only in þe erþe þey late her herte reste & delyte hem in sondry loue of men & wommen as þei come & gon nowe here on & nowe in another. And in ihu criste þei kon swetnes fynd. Or if þei ony tyme feel ought hit is so litel & so short for oþer worldly thoughte þt ar in hem. þat hit bryngith hem to no stabilnes. And thay arn like to a foule that men callen strucio. that hath wyngys and may not flee for chargid of body. So thay han understondyngis fasten and waken. and semis holy to mennys syght but thay wolden not flee vn to contemplacion in the loue of god. thay arn so chargid wt oþer affeccyous & veyne thoughtis.

13. Texts of Spiritual Guidance and Reflection. England; XV^{med}

Ff. i (paper) + 68 (fol. 1 being a medieval flyleaf) + i (paper). 310x211 (218x150 mm). Lines: 39. Ruling: ink. Quiring: generally 8s. Contemporary catchwords; quire letters and leaf numbers in the first half of quires. Binding, *s.* xvii, Hutchinson (rebacked *s.* xix^{med} and xxi^{in}): millboard covered in brown calf, outlined with double fillets, a further pair running vertically near the spine, a broken golden line along the board edges; 5 bands; 1 metal clasp.

Cosin V.i.12 (illustration: fol. 65v)

Amidst this collection of Latin monastic texts on the spiritual life—Ephraim the Syrian's, *Ad Monachos* plus the Isidorean *Commonitiuncula ad sororem* (2r–33v), extracts from homilies by Gregory the Great (33v–36r), sermons by Caesarius of Arles and Eusebius Gallicanus (36r–49v), the *De tribus habitaculis animae* generally associated with Patrick of Dublin (49v–52v), part of Hugh of Fouilloy's *De claustro anime* (52v–65r), and notes on different types of sins and the remedies for them (66r–68v)—appear one brief verse and one short prose work in English. The verse, appended to the explicit to *De claustro anime* at the bottom of 65r and, like it, written in red, expresses the mystery of transubstantiation in the manner of a riddle (found also in **no. 15**): "hit semeth whigth & hit is reed, hit is quyk & semeþ deed | hit is flessh & seemeth breed and veray god in his godhed" braced to "Da fidem domine" ("grant faith, O Lord") in the margin. The prose tract (which exactly fills the next page, 65v) is *The Bee* ("De natura apice") by Richard Rolle (d. 1349); this identifies three characteristics of that much-admired insect as morally worthy qualities for man to emulate, then takes two contrasting types of bird (well suited/ poorly suited to flight) as metaphors for service to God. Whereas many of Rolle's writings enjoyed formidable circulation, this work, by contrast, is extant in only two copies: the present one and that in Lincoln Cathedral MS 91, one of the manuscripts transcribed by Robert Thornton of East

Newton. Here it is isolated and anonymous, but there it appears amidst a run of Rolle's works and is identified as "Richardi heremite".

Our volume appears to be entirely the work of a single scribe writing a hybrid Secretary-Anglicana hand, who was also responsible for the rubrics and the numerous marginal headings. While plenty of these headings (particularly in the first three quires) simply say "nota" or "exemplum", many others name the subject or person they are flagging or the type of interpretation being offered ("moraliter"). However, they all but stop on 65r, and there is none for *The Bee*. The scribe prefaced several of the texts (including the last-mentioned) with an invocation to Jesus, Mary and (in all but the final case) Anna, placing their names above, before, or flanking the initial rubric (2r, 33v, 52v, 65v, 66r).

Each incipit and subsection is headed by a red initial flourished or embellished in the ink of the text and sometimes highlighted with the red of the rubric. Spirited and varied (those on 8v, 41v and 46v feature a profile head) rather than skilful, it seems highly likely that these, too, were the work of the scribe. All the red is vermilion; the yellow used to highlight certain letters is organic.

The earliest evidence for provenance comes in the form of two *s*. xv^2 inscriptions on the flyleaf (1r). The first states, "Iste liber constat Wilhelmo Crosse", in which the personal name has been supplied, mainly *in rasura*, by a second hand (all that remains visible of the original name(s) at this point is the top of a single ascender). Immediately below, the second hand has written the entire phrase, "Iste liber pertinett [sic] Wilhelmo crosse", confirming that that individual did indeed come to own the book. A William Cross is recorded at Oxford in the 1470s, another in Rockland, Norfolk, in 1479, but whether either of these is our man is an open question.

14. Lollard Dialogue. England; XIV^{ex}

Ff. 26: a medieval parchment booklet (fols. 6, 8, 10, 12, 15, 17, 19, 21) interleaved and bookended with *s.* xvi/xvii paper leaves (fols. i, ii, 1–5, 7, 9, 11, 13, 14, 16, 18, 20, 22–4). Parchment leaves: 264x162 (212x120) mm. Paper leaves: 266x190 (220x145) mm. Lines: 40. Ruling: ink on the parchment leaves, hard point on the paper ones. Binding, *s.* xvi–xvii: limp parchment wrapper, formerly secured with two ties (lost); reinforced with modern paper inserts in 1975–6.

Cosin V.iii.6 (illustration: fol. 6r)

This text explores the respective jurisdictions of pope and king, and the hierarchy of sacred and secular power more generally, via a dialogue between an English knight and a canon lawyer who has avowedly spent a long time at the papal curia: "[A] knigt of þe kinges of yngeland and a clerk of yngland þat was late comen fro þe courte, weren togider in a plase, So þat þe clerk bigan to speke of þe pope and in maner reproued þe knigt . . . ". Their exchanges (which range over such topics as the origin of papal authority, the Donation of Constantine, the material goods of the Church, the place of foreign priests within England, not to mention the fallibility of the clergy) favour the conclusion that papal authority is purely spiritual. Aligned with views of the controversial Oxford theologian John Wyclif (d. 1384), this work would seem to be a rare example of a Lollard tract that has survived in its original form as a pamphlet.

The work was transcribed on poor-quality parchment by a single scribe, using Anglicana formata (the concluding "Finis", formally penned in Textualis semi-quadrata, may have been added by a different hand). It is clearly subdivided, with each new intervention in the dialogue given a new paragraph and marked by a paraph in the margin and an ink initial, but is entirely without rubrication—even the paraphs are drawn in the ink of the text.

The earliest record of provenance is a *s.* xvi^{2} note on the final medieval page (21v): "Edward Robartsons booke seruaunt to Sir Nicholas Shelley knight capten' of [-blank-]". At this point, the tract was still a single quire. By c. 1600, however, it had been dramatically re-presented: it was interleaved with paper sheets bearing a line-by-line transcript of the medieval text, and a title page (1r) and dedicatory epistle to King James I (2r–3r) were prefixed, these both in the hand of William Crashaw. Here Crashaw, who describes himself as "Bachelour of Divinitye & preacher [subsequently "preacher of gods worde"] at the Temple", explains that he has been procuring and perusing ancient manuscripts, and suggests that the king should safeguard them as a record against papal falsehoods. Virulently anti-papist, William Crashaw (1572–1626), was preacher at the Temple Church, London, from 1605–13, by which time he had accumulated a substantial personal library. The greater part of his collection went (through the agency of the earl of Southampton) to St John's College, Cambridge.

knizt of þe kinges of yngeland & a clerk of
yngland þat was late comen fro þe courte were
togidir in a place. So þat þe clerk bigan to speke
of þe pope & in man' repreued þe knizt & said. I haue
grete wonder he said þat þe kinge & som of his counseil
& of his knizttes & oþer men of þe temporalte þat schuld be
gouerned bi holichirche. as bi þe pope & bi bishshopes &
bi þe clergy. melley þam of men of holichirch & of þair
gotes. in mani maners azaynes goddes lawe & azaines holi
chirch. for þai ne schuld nomaner mell oþe pope ne oþe clergi
for þai bene abouen all men. bi power zeuen to þaim
bi god him self als holi writt bereþ wittnes & þe lawe
canone also.

Yet sir said þe knizt þou spekes of a matere. þat clerkes
han oft moued amonge þe comone pupel. & þe pepel
haþ oft bene & es in a were & in dout þerof. And I my
self haue oft wondrid þat þe pope & þe clergi haþe
taken vpon hem. to supplant þe kinge þat es lorde
of his land & alldaie bene about more & more to ab
egge & lessen his power & his lordschip which as me þink
schuld nozgatt oþishalf god haue to done wiþ. ne
mell þam þerof. Neþeles bicause þat I am a litil letted
& vnderstonde somdele holi writt. I drede me þat I
mizt trist to mich to myne own witt in þis matere.
& so offend & gilt to god. And þou ert a memb' of holi
chirch a preste & semes a clerk cunnynge of clergi
I wold gladlich lerne of þe. bot it es oft sene þat
mony prestes & clerkes. þat beth gretelich auaunsid
gone wele arraied. & wele forþerid as þou dos þat bene
no cunnynge men of clergie ne of resoune. And þ'
for' I pray þe tell me what degre of scole þou has
þat I mow knowe wheþer þou be abul of cunnynge
to teche me in þis matere þat I am in dout.

Sir said þe clerk bicause þat I se þou has desyre to
lere I am rizt glad to tell þe þat þou ask' [illegible] all
be I vnworþi I am a doctor of decreeze & haue dwel
lid longe tyme in þe courte of rome & bene in office
wiþ þe pope.

In gode faiþ said þe knizt. I am wele paied. for I
hope to be wele taght bi þe of þat matere þat we haue

The popes Clergye think that kings may not meddle with them

The pope & his Clergye would supplant kings

ffor faythe no meyd ne meret hase.
To whome of mans reson.
Experiment hase.

De hoc sacramento dicit Ambrosius. Credere quade p̄ capimus: disputare artē p̄hibemus.

Calix. novi testamenti

Thow semest whyte. and art red.
Thow art fleshe. and semest bred
ye fairest myracle yat euer was.
To shew god and man. in so lytyl spa

15. Ecclesiastical Commonplace book. England (Bridlington); XVI^{in}

Ff. i (*s*. xix paper) + iii (*s*. xvii paper) + 84 + i (*s*. xix paper). Paper (watermark: ox head with snake, current xv^{ex}–xvi^{1}). 143x103 (90–105x70–85) mm. Lines: 14–20. Frame-ruled in hard point (red ink on 57v–58r, 67v–69r, 80v–81r, 82v). Quiring variable: 12, 18, 16 then 8s and 6s. Contemporary catchwords. Binding, *s*. xvii: millboard covered in brown calf, lightly speckled, outlined with triple blind fillets, a further triple blind fillet parallel to the spine; rolled with runs of squares along the board edges; 3 narrow bands; no clasp.

Cosin V.v.19 (illustration: fol. 72v)

Among texts and devotions for the Virgin Mary and St Anne, further prayers, scriptural and liturgical commentary, and other material (including four exempla for the miraculous properties of the words *In principio erat verbum*), this pocket-sized compendium features numerous items that relate specifically to the Augustinian priory of Bridlington, Yorkshire: two accounts of its foundation, an office for its saintly prior, John of Bridlington (d. 1379), his miracles, suffrages for him, an extract from Robert of Bridlington's commentary on Psalm 50, and notes relating to various members of the community. The rubric for the office for John of Bridlington ends with the name Thomas Ashby *canonicus* (23r); as this is written by the main hand of the rest of the book, it seems highly likely that the volume was the personal work of this man, who was ordained subdeacon in 1501, deacon and priest in 1503. The inclusion of an indulgence of Pope Julius II (sedit 1503–13) gives an approximate date-range for the compilation.

Thomas wrote passages of ordinary text in a clear cursive of Secretary type, upgrading to a larger version with more Textualis forms for certain rubrics and incipits, and to a bold Textualis semi-quadrata for others. His black ink (rich and dark) was gallo-tannic, his red ink vermilion. The only artwork in the volume, a drawing of the "Chalice of the New Testament" (72v), was done in the same red with details in the gallo-tannic black.

The texts are entirely in Latin except for a section on the mystery of the real presence in the Eucharist, where Latin *dicta* are interspersed with English verse (72r–73r). Thus *Sanctus gregorius dicit, Fides non habet meritum cui humana racio prebet experimentum* ("St Gregory says, Faith has no merit where human reason tests it") is followed by "In þe sacrament I am contyned bothe god and man. How þat is mans reson noght tell can. Lefe þerefor thy reson, And lett beleyfe þe leyd . . . ". And *De hoc sacramento dicit ambrosius, Credere quidem precipimus; disputare autem prohibimus. Calix. Noui Testamenti* ("Concerning this sacrament Ambrose says, indeed we command [you] to believe; moreover, we forbid [you] to dispute. Chalice of the New Testament") by "Thow semest whyte, and art red. Thow art fleshe, and semest bred . . . " (cf. **no. 13**), which ends with the warning that those who fail to believe in the real presence "To hell pytt shal þ[a] wend, Þare to be torment with owten end". After a sentence from Augustine's *De fide et symbolo* on the virtue of belief in such mysteries, the section ends with reiterated assertions that one should simply believe what the Church teaches. On the next pages (73v–74v), the mystic communions one experiences via the consecrated host, and their implications, are spelled out in five points attributed to Albertus episcopus (i.e. the Dominican Albert the Great, d. 1280), climaxing with "the whole Trinity" and its grace. It is an interesting reflection of Thomas Ashby's times that the vernacular should be harnessed uniquely for this dogmatic defence of a doctrine (transubstantiation) that had been contentious since Chaucer's lifetime, and to threaten those who might question the teachings of the institutional Church.

16. *Contemplations of the Dread and Love of God*; etc. England; XV^{med}

Ff. i (paper) + ii (*s*. xvii parchment) + 57 + i (paper). 200x140 (129x82) mm. Lines: 24. Ruling: ink. Quiring: 8s. Binding, *s*. xvii, Hutchinson (rebacked *s*. xx^{ex}): millboard covered in brown calf, lightly sprinkled, outlined with double blind fillets, two further pairs of blind fillets parallel to the spine; roll of squares and rectangles in gold along the board edges; 4 narrow bands; no clasp; remnants of the old spine-covering preserved when rebacked. Fols. 1 and 52–7 bear rust-stains from the metalwork of a single clasp from an earlier binding.

Cosin V.iv.6 (illustration: fol. 2r)

This volume contains two works: *Contemplations of the Dread and Love of God* (fols. 1r–48v) and *Contemplatio in Deo* (49r–56v). The first, which draws on the work of Richard Rolle and Brigit of Sweden (d. 1373), is believed to have been composed in the late fourteenth or early fifteenth century. Though addressed to all ranks of society, clerical and lay alike ("most nedfull eche man to haue, þat woll trauayl in gostliche werkes, and to all manere men and women they be full spedful to knowe, whether thei be religious or seculer", fol. 44v), it seems aimed more at layfolk than clergy ("þerfore to suche simple folk I woll shew a manere forme how by meditacion they mowe be steryd to deuocion and what manere preyer schall be to them needful", 44v). Four forms of love are distinguished whose specific qualities, along with the moral and devotional preconditions for them, are discussed in turn. The progression of themes is broadcast in a *kalendar* (table) of contents, written in red, which was avowedly designed to encourage reference and browsing—"þat þou mowe sone finde what mater þee pleseþ". Every subsection is designated by a letter of the alphabet ("A"–"Z" then "AB"), which then normally reappears at the top of each page throughout the section in question (no such letters were supplied on 13v–16v, sections "H"–"M"). The work concludes with a model devotion: meditation on individual elements of Christ's passion leads to a wide-ranging prayer of acclamation and contrition that climaxes with a plea to be able to love rightly, ending with a request for mercy for souls in purgatory. A marginal apparatus indicates sources (biblical and patristic) with varying degrees of precision ("Cassiodorus, de institutione monachorum l. 3"; "in quadam omelia"). Sixteen full copies are known, with excerpts appearing in a further twenty manuscripts, one of which is also in Durham (DCL, A.IV.22).

The second work, English versions of two portions of the *Speculum Ecclesiae* by Edmund of Abingdon (d. 1240), is arranged in seven sections, one prescribed for use before each of the canonical hours except Lauds (normally said in tandem with Matins) (cf. **no. 17**). Thus the first commences, "Bifore matynes þe shalt þenk furst of þe natiuite. And afterward of þe passion . . .". These structured meditations on pairs of events from Christ's life and afterlife, invite—implicitly and explicitly—extended contemplation of his human and divine nature for, as the preface declares, "contemplacion [of] god hym self is þe hyghest degre of contemplacion and þat may be in two maneres, oon withoute in his manheed. And an ooþer within in his blessyd godhed".

The volume is the work of a single scribe, writing Anglicana with a few Secretary features, upgrading to Textualis semi-quadrata for rubrics; up to 23r, but not thereafter, selected ascenders and capitals in the top lines were calligraphically extended. In the first text, the main divisions are marked by blue initials flourished in red, the numerous subdivisions by paraphs, alternately red then blue until 39r, red alone thereafter. The red is vermilion, the blue azurite. The space reserved for an initial heading the second text remained unfilled, though rubrication was accomplished (in red alone) throughout.

Both texts were corrected and annotated by one hand later in the fifteenth century. Casual jottings added *s.* xvi^1 include "John Weston miles vic" [or "vir"] (15v), "Thomas Weston miles vic/vir" (50r) and "Thomas umpton Miles vic/vir" (48r), this last conceivably the Thomas Unton/Umpton who was sheriff of Berkshire and Oxfordshire and was knighted at the coronation of Anne Boleyn in May 1533, dying three months later. The earliest clear evidence of ownership is the inscription "thys ys Rob[er]t whytneys boke", written on 49v in an elongated Italic, *s.* xvi^2: this is perhaps one of the men of that name from the Whitney family of Whitney, Herefordshire, who were alive then.

Jhc

In the begynnynge and endynge of alle goode
werkys. Worship and thankynge be to almyghty
god. maker and beyer of all mankynde by-
gynner and ender of all goodnesse. With oute
whoos yifte and help: no maner vertu is. ne
may be. whether it be in thoght. wil. or dede.
What eu[er] we thanne þat be synfull thenke or
do: speke or wryte. þat may turne in to profyte of
mannys soule: to god oonlyche be the worship
þat all grace sent. to us no preysynge ne þankynge
for of us. with oute hym cometh noght. but
filthe and synne. Now thanne goode god of
his endles myght and plentevous goodnesse:
graunte me grace to thenke sumwhat of his dere love:
and how he shulde be loved. of that love summe
wordes to wryte. whiche mowe be to hys worship
to [illegible] mede: and profitable to þe rederes. vbi p[ri]n[ci]p[iu]m vu

Amonge all creatures whiche god of his endles
mercy made. was ther neue noon that he
so loved. as he loved man [illegible] whom he made
to rejoyse eue lastynge blysse: in the stede of Angelis
whiche fellyn from blysse doun in to helle. Thanne
good god loved so man þat for as moche man had for-
fetyd that blysse thorugh the synne of Adam. he

Iste liber sequens fuit compositus in latino sermone per quendam fratrem minorem cardinalem nobilem doctorem Bonaventuram nomine postea translatus est in linguam anglicanam pro minoribus latinum non intelligentibus per reverendum dominum Walterum Hilton nomine in amore dei valde devotum. How a man schal haue aftir passioun in medio [illegible]

We wondier of oure self aght vs to be if we bethoght vs in
herte of ye grete vnmesurable loue þat god to vs hath schewed.
And of ye grete vnkyndnesse þat we don hym agayn for his
good dede. ffor if oure lord liffed vs so mekil þat to oure
kynde so knitted he wolde be þat nede he wolde for vs tholyne but
if we make it oure self. So mekil more ilk on of vs aght to opnen
his herte ful wide vnto so dere a frend & so kynde our lif to hym
þat no wordes wele ne wo myght it fram hym departe. Þerfore þat
man is more þan wood þat schulde therfore forsake when it is to hym
so largeli profred for þat thing þat is but stynkande filthe. Goddis
sone of heven ihesu tok not oure flessch as to folwe oure flesschly wil
But als he hym self whiles he was wiþ vs erþe in oure kynde suffred peynes & passions in hise flessch wilfully for vs. And ȝet
nevertheles with god his fadir was ay his soule. Ryght so schal man
pyne his flessch & agaynstonden flesschly willes ȝif he be bounden
þer to & ȝet liften vp his spirit on heighte be thoght & desire in our
lord ihesu likyng for to haue. But wonder blynd is man þat knowes
not hym self. Hou þat his soule wiþ oute comparisoun is nobler gentiler
heigher & fayrer in kynde þan is ye flessch. For it is ye ymage of god
made to his lyknesse. And þerfore as a fool he spendes alle his wittes
& his myghtes in fulfillyng of þat thing þat his flessch ȝernith & forge-
teth his soule as if he hadde non. He hath no routhe of it ne reweth
ne rechez to kepe it in god myght so fere. He hath no pite of it ne liste
for to rayse it out of synne, ne to seke helpe of ihesu crist ȝif it so
be þat no thing be so plesand ne so lighte so wele so saue as is
ye grace of ihesu crist. ffor wete þat it is only ye lif and ye hele & ye wele-
fare of ye soule. Untel tonge ye heie fadir of heven wretched man þat wolde
wit non other for bye mannes soule to blisse but only thurgh ded of his awn
dereworthi sone ihesu crist. ffor whi for noghte þat ani man myght do he sulde
neuere haue seen ye fadres face if ihesu crist had not be ded & for oure synnes
be rysen vp. on bo nyght & day for to calle vs & pray vs to his loue þat
we schulde loue hym agayn bycause þat loved vs so mekel. Wonder is it þat
of blyndnesse of ye soule þat is so fer in hyr kynde þat no thing nel styre
hyr to do any thing agaynes hys wil. And ȝet nevertheles for he loves fre
to seke [illegible] lif of ihesu þat boght hyr wiþ his blood [illegible] folowe aftir [illegible]

17. *The Privity of the Passion*; *The Prickynge of Love*. England; XV^in

Ff. i (*s.* xvii paper) + 2 (parchment flyleaves, foliated "I"–"ii") + 66 + 2 (parchment endleaves, foliated "iii"–"iv") + i (*s.* xvii paper). 226x154 (178x117) mm. Full grid of ink rulings in quire I; frame-ruled thereafter. Lines: 39–43. Quiring: 8s (the last now reduced to 3). Contemporary catchwords. Quire letter and leaf number on the leaves in the first half of quires. Binding, *s.* xviii, Hutchinson: millboard covered in speckled calf; outlined with a double blind fillet, with a further pair of double verticals parallel to the spine, a rolled pattern along the hinge, roll of squares and rectangles in gold along the board edges; 4 narrow bands; 1 metal clasp.

Cosin V.iii.8 (illustration: fol. 16r)

This volume once held more than the two works it now contains: the last quire is imperfect and offsets on what is now the final verso (66v) show that the next page was adorned with flourished initials—implying the incipit to a new text or conceivably a *tabula* (a listing of contents). The surviving texts, *The Privity of the Passion* (fols. 1r–14v) and *The Pryckinge of Love* (16r–66v, its last few lines lost), are both fourteenth-century English versions of Latin works that were popularly if erroneously credited to St Bonaventure (d. 1274)—respectively the *Meditationes vitae Christi* (chs. 74–92) and the *Stimulus amoris* (both now ascribed to c. 1300, the former attributed to a Franciscan called Jacobus/James from San Gimignano, the latter by the Franciscan James of Milan). The prefatory rubric to *The Pryckinge* identifies Walter Hilton (d. 1396) as the translator (whether he was genuinely responsible is debated).

The Latin originals enjoyed wide circulation, and English renderings were also popular. Five other English versions of the passion section of the *Meditationes* are known and, while none of these is extant in more than a handful of copies (with a total of five witnesses, the one found in our volume is the best represented), the version of the whole text done by Nicolas Love (d. 1423/4) at the beginning of the fifteenth century (*Mirrour of the Blessed Lyf of Jesus Crist*) survives in over fifty copies. The *Prickynge* is extant fully in eleven manuscripts and partially in a further six.

With direct appeals to the reader and emotive language, *The Privity of the Passion* works through events from the Last Supper to the post-resurrection appearances, embellishing and glossing the biblical narrative in ways calculated to incite affective piety—not least lingering over the torments that Christ endured. The rubrics of several of the earlier sections specify times for the meditation in question in relation to the canonical hours ("A meditatioun for þe houre of prime . . . ", "at þe hour of vnderne [terce] . . . ", " . . . in þe hour of midday . . . ", " . . . in þe hour of noon . . . ", " . . . atwix noon & evensong", " . . . in þe houre of compleyne", "A meditation after compleyn . . . "), linking the devotional exercise to the cycle of the daily office for those in religious orders, for the laity to that of the Little Office of the Virgin in Books of Hours (see **nos. 20–2**). Equally, the biblical events themselves are sometimes tied to the same framework: "al þis þat he suffred in þe hour of mateyn, of prime and of vnderne . . . " (5r). *The Prickynge of Love*, which offers a modestly simplified version of the Latin original, begins with a series of meditations on the passion, larded with teaching on the basic tenets of Christianity (Chapters 1–9), then moves on to explore the nature of earthly spirituality and the workings of the contemplative life (Chapters 10–33); there follow an exchange between the mortified flesh and God (Chapters 34–5), then reflections on the Pater noster (36), Ave Maria (37), and Salve Regina (38); the final chapter (39) is "Of þe stat of blissid soules in hefnly Ierusalem".

Our manuscript was written by a single scribe who was also responsible for its rubrics. Both surviving incipits are introduced by an historiated initial/vignette, the first featuring Christ carrying the cross (an episode treated within *Privity*'s third meditation, fol. 5r), the second showing his crucified corpus (central to the first nine chapters of *Prickynge*); the incipit here may have been modified (from "Al for wondrid" to "For wondred") in order to have an initial letter whose shape suited a crucifixion. Be that as it may, both images accord with the texts in general terms in fostering empathy for Christ's sufferings while, more specifically, they support the injunction in the preface to *Privity* that, in order to open one's soul to the spiritual blessings available through meditating on the passion, one should strive to visualize its various stages.

Subsections are marked by blue initials flourished in red. All the red (for rubrics and in the historiations as well as for flourishing) is vermilion, all the blue azurite; in addition, the historiations feature a copper green, an organic brown, white lead, and gold leaf (untooled).

The earliest evidence of provenance is a name added to the top of 1r. Although this is now very faint, the same inscription was written by the same hand on the title page of a copy of Gabriel Putherbeus / Dupuyherbach, *Theotinus*, printed in Paris in 1549 (DUL, Routh XII.E.12), confirming the name as "Jo. Fenum" and providing a *terminus post quem* for his activities; four manuscripts in the British Library are reported to bear the same name.

Malbodio monastio. sce aldegundis ūgis. xviij. kl.
i c. Apd' tciā ciuitate eraclea. natal' scoꝝ decebr.
Anīte. clemētini theodoti. ꝫ philomini. Alexan
drie. sci serapionis. Que psecutores sub decio pncip
crudelissimis affecerūt suppliciis. Ita ut oēs ei iunctu
ras membroꝝ pius solueretur. de sinibz eius pcipitarē
ut sic xpi martir efficeretur. xvij. kl. decēb.
d Apd' nolā cāpanie urbē. natal' bi felicis epi
Qui a xv. etatis sue anno miraculoꝝ glā insig
nis fuit. ꝫ sub marciano pside cū aliis triginta mrtm
cōpleuit. Ipo die. sci eugenii. q' apd' pagū parisia
cēse cōsūmato mri cursu. bē passionis coronā
pcepit a dño. Itē eode die. sci macuti epi ꝫ cfessor
ix e Lugduni. natal' sci eutherii xvj. kl. decēb.
cōfessoris. Qui ex nobilissimo senatoꝝ ordine ad
religiosā uitā habitūqz cōuersus diu intersepta spe
lunce sponte clausus ꝫ seruiuit. Deinde ad pfatā
urbē reuelāte angelo in pōtificali cathedra sollēp
nit collocat' ē. Eode die sci edmūdi archiepi ꝫ cf.
f Apd' alexandriā. bi dionisii epi. xv. kl. decēb.
Hic in multis sepe cōfessionibz satis clar'. ꝫ p
passionū tormētoꝝ qz diuersitate magnific' extites q
cunt ualeriani ꝫ galieni imperatoꝝ tēporibz. Ciuitate

18. Martyrology. England; XIV/XV

Ff. ii (*s.* xvii paper) + 68 (plus unfoliated parchment supplement slip sewn to 12v) + i (*s.* xvii paper). 205x145 (160x105) mm. Lines: 23. Ruling: ink. Quiring: 8s then 10s. Contemporary catchwords within ornamented scrolls. Binding, *s.* xvii, Hutchinson (rebacked, *s.* xix^{med}): millboard covered with brown calf, divided by pairs of fillets into four concentric panels, the second and the outermost of which are tooled with interlocking foliate flourishes (cf. **no. 19**), the other two plain (bar triangles of blind-tooled patterning in the four corners of the innermost one); chevron pattern rolled along the board edges; 4 narrow bands; 1 metal clasp.

Cosin V.iii.17 (illustration: fol. 60v)

This martyrology (a day-by-day listing of saints, starting on 24 December with "the vigil for the nativity of the Lord") is the second recension of that compiled by Usuardus of Saint-Germain-des-Prés (d. 877), enhanced with a substantial stratum of British and, to a lesser extent, northern French *sancti*, those on the selected opening ("xviij kl' decembris" to "xiij kl' decembris", i.e. 14–19 November) being Malo/Maclou/Machutus of Wales and Brittany (15 November), Edmund of Abingdon (16 November), Hilda of Whitby, and Hugh of Lincoln (both 17 November). Inserted into the text of our copy at the appropriate points by a contemporary annotator were the translation of Richard of Chichester (16 June, 32v), and the feasts of Anne (26 July, 39v) and Kenan of Damleag/Duleek (24 November, 62r), this last specified as an observance *in hybernia* ("in Ireland"). St Anne, celebration of whose feast was promoted in England in 1383, provides a *terminus post quem* for these early supplements.

The original text was written by a single hand in Textualis semi-quadrata: if this formal script was chosen to reflect and project the sacrality of the subject matter, the effect is rather undermined by the density with which the writing was applied to the page as also by its irregularities and forward-leaning ductus. Equally, the visual solemnity is counterbalanced by the grotesque faces with which the scribe ornamented several of the catchwords and one descender (49r). Each new day is marked by an initial, alternately red then blue, the very first (1r) of both colours; a few of the blue initials were crudely flourished in red. The red is vermilion, the blue azurite (unusually granular and thickly applied—a good illustration of the fact reported by the Tuscan artist Cennino Cennini (d. 1427) that the less this pigment is ground, the darker and richer its hue).

The earliest evidence for provenance is an *ex dono* inscription on the final page (68v) which records the gift of the book in 1514 by Christopher Massingberd, canon of Lincoln Cathedral, the recipient unspecified. Massingberd, who took up his canonry in 1512, went on to hold various appointments in the diocese and at the cathedral of Lincoln, including (from 1533) its chancellorship; he died in 1553.

19. Manual (Use of Sarum, noted). England; XIV[ex]

Ff. ii (*s*. xvii paper) + 67 (foliated "1"–"11", "11*"–"66") + iv (*s*. xvii paper). Fol. 11* is an inserted parchment slip. 185x136 (145–52x98) mm. Lines: 29. Ruling: ink. Quiring: 8s (Qq. I, III and V now imperfect). Binding, Hutchinson *s*. xvii[med]: millboard covered with brown calf, divided by pairs of fillets into four concentric panels, the second and the outermost tooled with interlocking foliate flourishes (cf. **no. 18**); 11 pairs of fillets compartmentalize the spine; chevron pattern roll along the board edges; 4 narrow bands; 1 metal clasp.

Cosin V.iii.21 (illustration: fols. 11v & 11*v)

Containing the services and formulae for priests administering the sacraments—the blessing of salt and water (1r–2v), catechumens (3r–4v), blessing a font (4v–9v), baptism (9v–11v), marriage (11v–18v), visiting the sick (18v–23r), extreme unction (23r–30v), commendation of souls for use beside a body (30v–39r), vigil of the dead (39r–60v), commendation of souls for use in choir or chapter (60v–62r), and burial (62r–66v)—this manual has seen heavy use, as the weathering and the loss of leaves attest.

The texts are entirely in Latin except for the nuptial vows, which are given in English (cf. **no. 24**) (although the priest's aforegoing questions to the couple were to have been posed, the rubric specifies, *in lingua materna*, the relevant wording was nonetheless supplied in Latin: "Vis habere hanc mulierem in sponsam . . . "). A couple of generations after the book had been made, alternative versions of the vernacular vows were supplied on an inserted slip. Where the original text for the man read, "ych N take þe N to my beddede [sic] wyf the to loue worschepe holde & kepe in sekenesse and in helthe as a man schal his wyf & alle oþ*er* for the leue & forsake, and to þe onlyche holde . . . " (12r), the replacement offered: "I N take N to my weddede wife to haue And to holde for fayrer for fowler for bettur for wors for Richer for porer in sykenes and in hele for thys time forward . . . " (11*v). For the woman's original "ych N take þe N to my weddede hosobonde to the to be obeyssaunt and serue, loue and worchepe holde & kepe in sekenesse and in helthe as a woman schal housebonde &

alle othere for the leue and to þe onlyche holde & take . . . " was substituted "I N take þe N to my webbe [sic] husbond to haue & to hold for feyrer for fowlur for bettur for wors for Richer for porer in sekenes & in helþe to be lawfulliche & boxum in bedde and at burde from þis time forward til dethe us dep*ar*te as holi church' it well ordeyne & þer to I pligth þe my truthe".

Chaucer's Wife of Bath famously "housbondes at chirche dore she hadde five" (l. 460). The standard rubrics, as given in the present manual (and in **no. 24**), duly locate the formalities of the marriage itself (checking for impediments, the exchange of vows, the blessing and accepting of the ring) *ante ostium ecclesie*. Only thereafter does the couple progress to the altar step for prayers, then back into the choir for the nuptial mass.

The beginning of the book is marked by a decorated initial plus an all-round border in blue, purple and gold (badly damaged), the principal divisions by initials in blue or mauve on gold (or vice versa) plus border extensions in blue, mauve, orange, green, and gold, all qualitatively modest. Subdivisions are headed by blue initials flourished in red. All the reds (in decoration, flourishing, rubrics, and staves alike) are vermilion; the pinks and purples are organic, the orange is red lead, the green copper-based, the blue azurite, the white is white lead, the black gallo-tannic.

There is no evidence of provenance prior to the acquisition of the book by George Davenport (for whom, see **no. 1**).

[...]tuus est. Ipse autem tenens manum eius eleuauit
eum: et surrexit. Et cum introisset domum: discipu
li eius secreto interrogabant eum. Quare nos non
potuimus eicere eum: Et dixit illis. Hoc genus

Ecce conuenimus hic fr[...] coram [...]
et omnibus sanctis in facie ecclesie ad coniungendum duo cor
pora scilicet huius viri et huius mulieris vt amodo sint vnum
corpus et due anime in fide et in lege dei ad promerendum
simul vitam eternam quicquid ante hoc fecerit adiu
ro vos per patrem et filium et spiritum sanctum vt si quis et vobis
aliquid sciat quare ista legittime conuenire non possint
nunc illud confiteatur

I N take N to my wedded wife to haue and to hold
for fairer for fowler for bettur for wors for richer
for porer in sekenes and in hele for thys time for
ward til dethe vs depte as holichurche well ordeyn
& þer to I plighþ þe my truthe

I N take þe N to my webbe husbond to haue & to
hold for feirer for fowlur for bettur for wors for
richer for porer in sekenes & in helpe to be ballfulli
che & boxum in bedd and at burde from þis time
forward til dethe us depte as holichurch it well
ordeyne & þer to I plighþ þe my truthe

[...] Post hec dicat [...]
[...] ad virum cunctis audientibus. N. Vis ha
bere hanc mulierem in sponsam et eam diligere hono

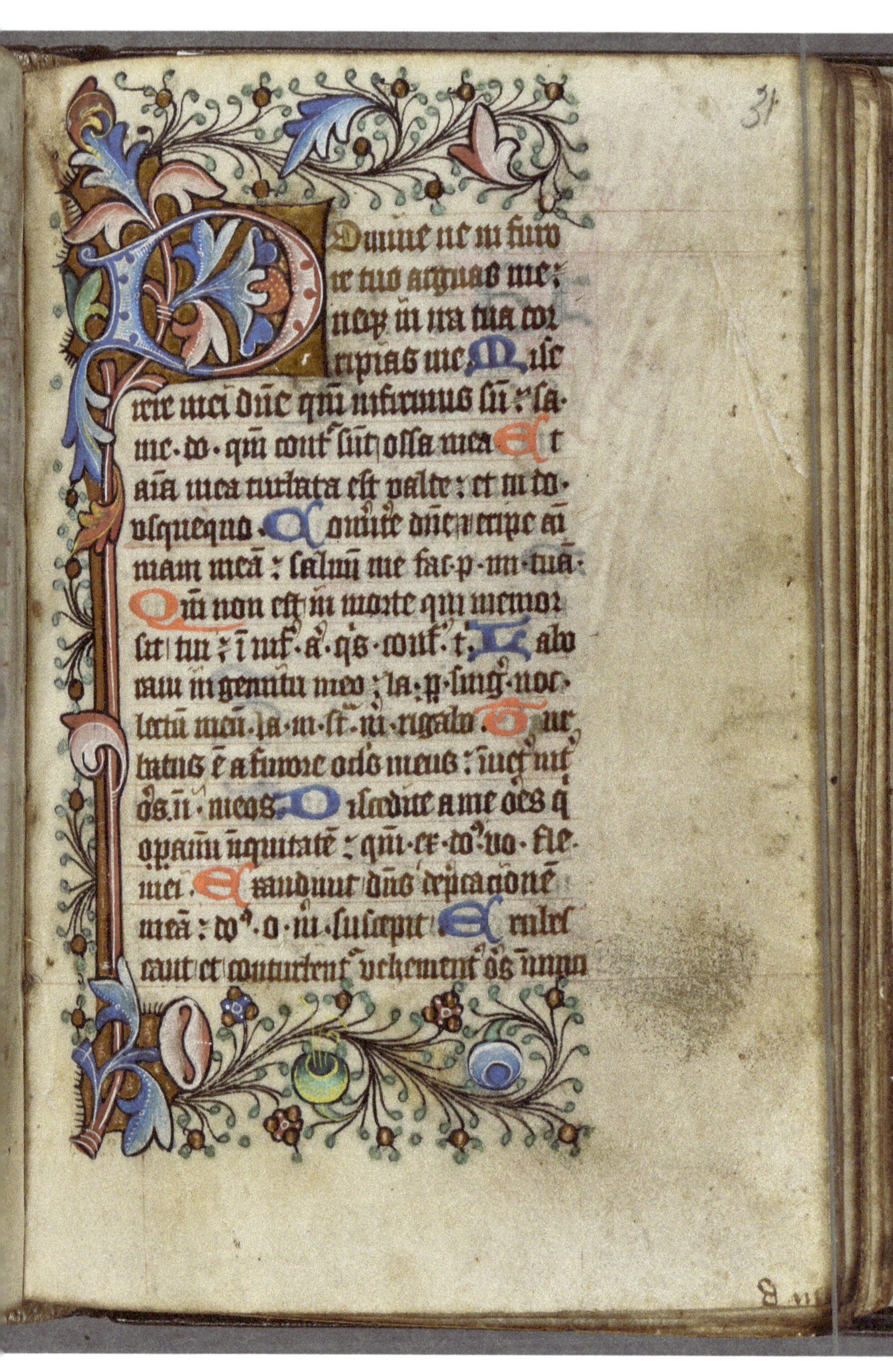

Domine ne in furo
re tuo arguas me;
neqz in ira tua cor
ripias me. Mise
rere mei dne qm infirmus sum: sa-
na me do. qm cont'bata sunt ossa mea. Et
aia mea turbata est valde: et tu do.
usquequo. Convertere dne eripe ai
mam meam: salvum me fac p. mi. tua.
Qm non est in morte qui memor
sit tui: i inf. a. q's conf. t. Labo
ravi in gemitu meo; la. p. sing. noc.
lectum meum. la. m. st. m. rigabo. Tur
batus e a furore ocls meus: inveteravi
ins. i. inimicos. Discedite a me oes q
opamini iniquitatem: qm ex. do. vo. fle.
mei. Exaudivit dns deprecaconem
meam: do. o. m. suscepit. Erubes
cant et conturbentur vehement' oes inimi

20. Book of Hours (Use of Sarum). England; XV^2

Ff. i (modern parchment) + 82 (two unfoliated leaves, then 80 foliated ones) + i (modern parchment). 136x96 (83x49) mm; Lines: 19. Ruling: ink (red). Quiring: 8s (Qq. I, III and VII now imperfect). Contemporary catchwords, some within scrolls; quire letter plus leaf number on rectos of leaves in the first half of quires. Binding, *s.* $XX^{1/2}$: brown calf over pasteboard; 4 bands.

Moriarty 1 (illustration: fol. 31r)

Although this much-used book now lacks its calendar and has suffered other losses, sufficient survives to show a strong connection with Lichfield (and Shrewsbury): the only "local" figures to feature in the suffrages are (in order of appearance) Chad, founder and first bishop of Lichfield, Thomas Becket, and Winifrid, who was culted at Shrewsbury (whence her relics had been translated in 1138); Chad is the only individual to appear in all of the alternate litanies (invariably heading the confessors); moreover, his name is one of only two that are written in red (the other being that of Winifrid).

The rebus on fol. 1r (a roe deer inscribed "ger" reposing before a towered wall) links the book to Roger Walle (d. 1488), who was, *inter alia*, Master of St Andrew's Hospital, Denhall, Cheshire (from 1436), canon and prebendary of St John's Chester (1438) then of Lichfield (1440), archdeacon of Stafford then Coventry (1442), and prebendary of Eccleshall, Lichfield (1449). Roger can be associated via his rebus and inscriptions with a number of manuscripts, including copies of John Gower's *Vox Clamantis* (Oxford, Bodleian Library, Digby 138), Ranulf Higden's *Polychronicon* (Cambridge, Trinity College, O.5.12), and both the metrical and the prose lives of Henry V by Thomas Elmham (Glasgow University Library, Hunter U.5.3 (263); London, College of Arms, Arundel 15), some of which he transcribed himself. The present book of hours received early additions both at front and back—"[S]alvator mundi saluum me fac . . . " (fols. i verso–ii recto), "Salue mater helena constantini regis | Ave felix femina . . . " (fol. ii verso), and "[A]ve plena gratia beata maria | [A]ve dei genitrix ave virgo [pia] | [A]ve rosa lilium paradisi via . . . " (fol. 80v)—done by three different hands, none of which, however, is obviously that of Roger himself.

The main text is the work of two scribes (the second commencing at the Commendation of Souls, halfway down 72r). The major textual divisions in the book are marked by decorated initials with border bars and foliate extensions (the selected example is that for the Penitential Psalms, 31r); secondary sections are headed by golden letters on red and blue panels enhanced by spray-work, all other subdivisions by blue initials flourished in red. The pigments used were vermilion, red lead, lead-tin yellow, copper-based and vergaut greens (the latter confected from indigo plus lead-tin yellow), azurite, white lead, and gold leaf.

The last private owner of the volume, as attested by the bookplate inside the front board, was Ambrose Moriarty (1870–1949), priest in Shrewsbury from 1894, bishop of Shrewsbury 1934–49.

21. Book of Hours (Use of Sarum). Bruges, XV^{in} (1409)

Ff. 133. 206x139 (118x69) mm. Lines: 23. Ruling: ink. Quiring: 8s (plus inserted singletons bearing miniatures). Contemporary catchwords. Binding, xvi^{in}: wooden boards covered in dark leather, stamped with (front) Augustus and the Tiburtine Sibyl, and (back) SS. Thomas apostle and Paul, holding set-square and sword respectively, flanking a tree; below is a shield with the initials "LW" (J. B. Oldham, *Blind Panels of English Binders*, Misc. 2 and ST 48); 5 bands; 2 clasps (the clasps themselves lost).

Ushaw 10 (illustration: fol. 25v)

This charming volume, its principal divisions prefaced by full-page miniatures and enlivened by border bars with drolleries, ends (132v) with a colophon in the hand of the single scribe which records that it was written in Bruges by John Heineman, further noting that he finished his work on 26 January "1408" (new style 1409). Sixteen of the twenty-four miniatures were done on singletons and inserted into the text at the appropriate points; however, the first eight (for the suffrages and a prayer to the Trinity) were painted onto the relevant pages within the written quires and are thus interwoven with Heineman's contribution. As all the miniatures are in the same manner, using the same pigments, the work and the style can be localized to Bruges. The pigments employed were: red—vermilion plus organic, vermilion plus red lead, red lead alone; dark red—organic; pink—organic plus white lead; brown—ochre; yellow—lead-tin yellow; green—vergaut (indigo plus lead-tin yellow); blue—lapis lazuli (of varying quality but never mixed with azurite) with indigo for detailing; white—white lead; black—carbon, indigo (for dark shading); plus gold leaf and gold ink ("shell gold").

A number of manuscripts with closely related decoration and script have been assembled around our book to form the so-called Ushaw Group of illuminated manuscripts. Collectively these volumes reveal the "production line" nature of some book-making and decoration at Bruges

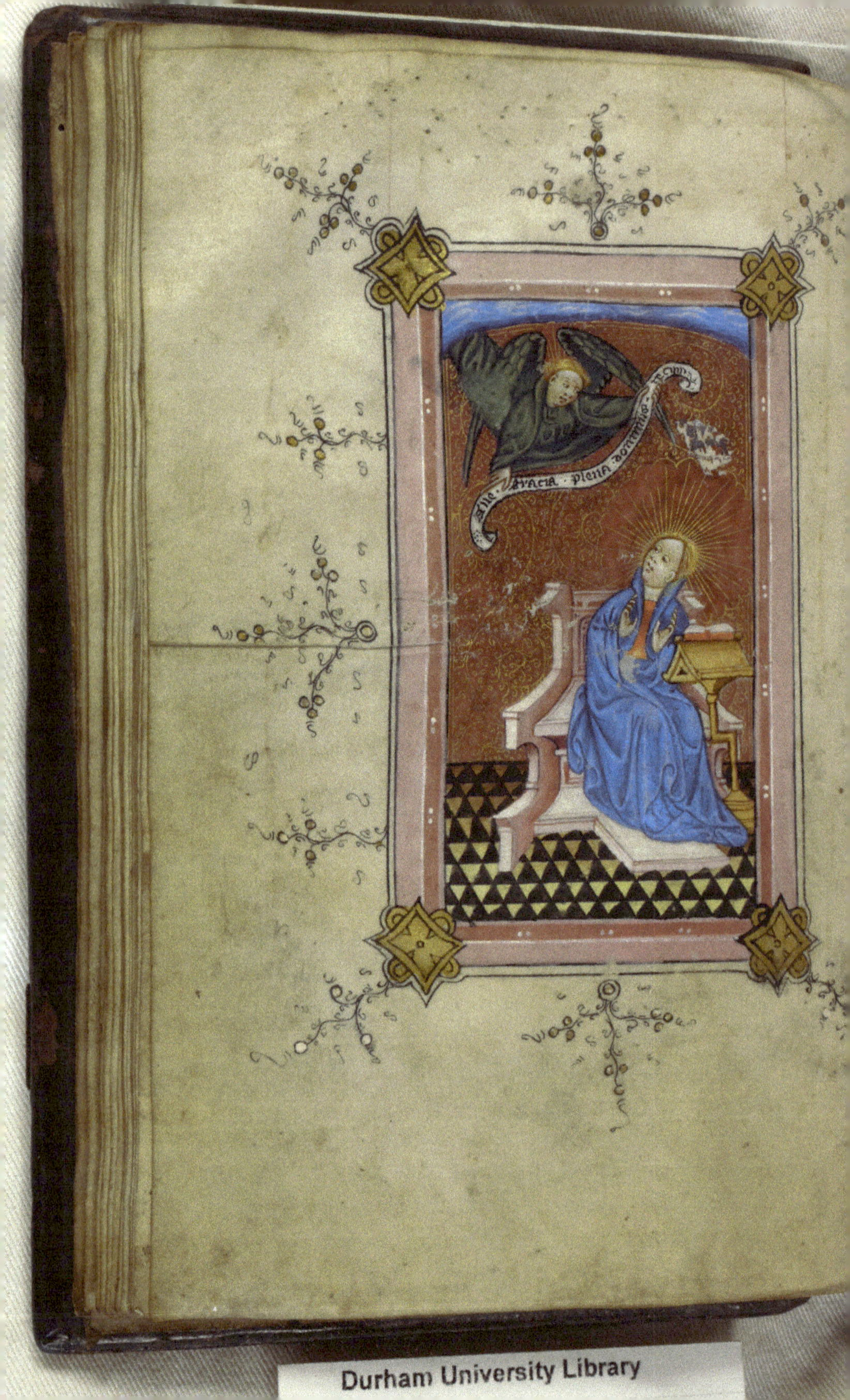
Ave · gracia · plena · dominus ·
Durham University Library

c. 1400. They also highlight how many such manuscripts were made for the English market (cf. **no. 22**).

Ushaw 10, of Sarum Use, is itself a case in point, and that it had reached and was being used in England from an early date is demonstrated by the numerous additions in English in fifteenth- and early sixteenth-century hands. On the first leaves were added a 48-line verse supplication to Henry VI, known only from this manuscript ("O blyssyd kynge so full of vertue | þe flowr of all knyghthod þat neuer was sylyd | . . . | Thys I besech at my request | Now swet kyng henre praye for me", 1r–2r), and an English translation of *O intemerata*, one of the two most frequently-occurring Marian prayers in *horae* ("[O] mary the modyr of god synguler madyn vnfylid and blyssid withowtyn end, To whom no comparison may be mayde. Thow art kyndly the tempyll of god . . . ", 2r–v). After the calendar was inserted a tripartite (Trinitarian) Marian prayer ("*Ex omnipotencia patris.* O swytte blyssyd lade as thow arte moste myght nexte god in hewyn & in herthe . . . *Ex sapientia filii.* O glorius lady as thow arte moste wytty nexte god in hewyn & in herthe . . . *Ex beningnitate* [sic] *spiritus sancti.* O gracius lady as thow arte moste lufly nexte god in hewyn and in herthe . . . and gytte me grace and lufe of god in the oure of my dethe Ave Maria", 9r). To blank spaces in the suffrages were added: the devotion, "haue in mynde a thousand Aues" (11r); another devotion ("If yu be in dedely syn or in trubulacon or in ony deses goy to the kerke and falle on your knes before the rode and beseyk hym meykly that he wald have mercy . . . And knaw þu for certann þat þ[i] praeyr schal be graciusly hard and notte falleyd") with English rubrics and Latin (psalm) incipits (12v–13r); and "In nomine iesu omne genu flectatur . . . To the blysyd trinite say thresse that follows . . . "—a set of short Latin prayers, all but the first with rubrics in English, the last crediting its *oraison* ("Ave sanctissime maria mater . . . ") with bringing "Elevyne thousande yere off trewe indulgence" (14v–15r). On the final leaf of the book (133r) was inscribed the prayer, "Lorde iesu cryst for the bytternes wych thow sufferde in þ[i] most bitter passion . . . hawe mercy oppen my synfull sawle in the departynge fro my wrytchyde body. In nomine patris [etc.]."

Inserted at the bottom of the calendar page for January (3r) was the couplet, "After the blak pryme what yere so it be | the next sondy say, laus tibi domine", with another in the same hand at the bottom of that for April (4r): "The next sonday aftre the blak pryme | shall be pasche day, how so it tyme." This mnemonic for the date of Easter is followed by "quod" then a sketch of a chess rook plus "cliff"—the rebus of Sir Brian Ro(u) cliffe (d. 1494), a lawyer who became third (1452) then second (1483) Baron of the Exchequer and was lord of the Manor of Cowthorp near Wetherby, Yorkshire, whose parish church he rebuilt (consecrated 1458). If the "magnum primarium nuper dominae Margaretae Burgh ex dono dominae Elizabeth Elyngham" ("great primer recently belonging to Lady Margaret Burgh by gift of Lady Elizabeth Elyngham") that he bequeathed to his son can be identified with the present book, then it had presumably descended from a relative of his mother, Joan, daughter of Thomas Burgh of Kirtlington, Nottinghamshire. Brian Roucliffe's family is connected to another extant Book of Hours—the rather more modest, English-made Edinburgh University Library, 41, to whose calendar was added note of the marriage in April 1464 between his eldest son, John, and the then-infant Margaret Plumpton, granddaughter of Sir William Plumpton (1404–80).

22. Book of Hours (Use of Sarum). Bruges; XV^{in}

Ff. 81 (fols. 78–81 medieval endleaves). 210x148 (134x83) mm. Lines: 26. Ruling: ink (red). Quiring: 8s and 6s (plus inserted singletons bearing miniatures). Contemporary catchwords; quire letters and leaf numbers on rectos in the first half of quires. Binding, *s.* xv^{in}: bevelled wooden boards, covered with leather (pink colouring preserved on turn-ins), lost from the spine and back; 4 double bands; board channels alternately long, short, long, short, all at 90° to the spine; 3 strap and pin fastenings, ?reworked at different dates, the original straps lacking; the rear pastedown lifted, the front pastedown lost.

Ushaw 14 (illustration: fol. 7v)

This volume, like Ushaw 10 (**no. 21**), is another of the many *horae* that were made in Bruges for the English market. Again like Ushaw 10, it is linked through the style of its miniatures and the hand of its scribe to other books, collectively known as the Beaufort Group (after British Library, Royal 2 A.xviii). Although Ushaw 14 and 10 have most major textual items in common, the various subsidiary prayers unique to one as opposed to the other underline how much variety was possible in such books—and hence in private devotion—even when mass-produced. Correspondingly, while Ushaw 10 has suffrages both as a discrete section at the front of the book (featuring Christopher, George, Thomas Becket, John the Baptist with John the Divine, Mary Magdalene, Katherine with Margaret, and Anne, all prefaced by a miniature), and following Lauds in the Office of the Virgin (for Michael, John the Baptist, Peter and Paul, Andrew, Stephen, Laurence, George, Thomas Becket, Nicholas, Mary Magdalene, Katherine), the present manuscript only has the latter (for John the Baptist, Peter, Andrew, Laurence, Thomas Becket, Nicholas, Mary Magdalene, Katherine, Margaret, and All Saints). Thomas Becket, who was almost invariably included in the litanies of Sarum *horae* made on the continent (and is duly present among the martyrs in that of Ushaw 10), is, unusually, absent from that of the present book (though all three of his feasts feature in the

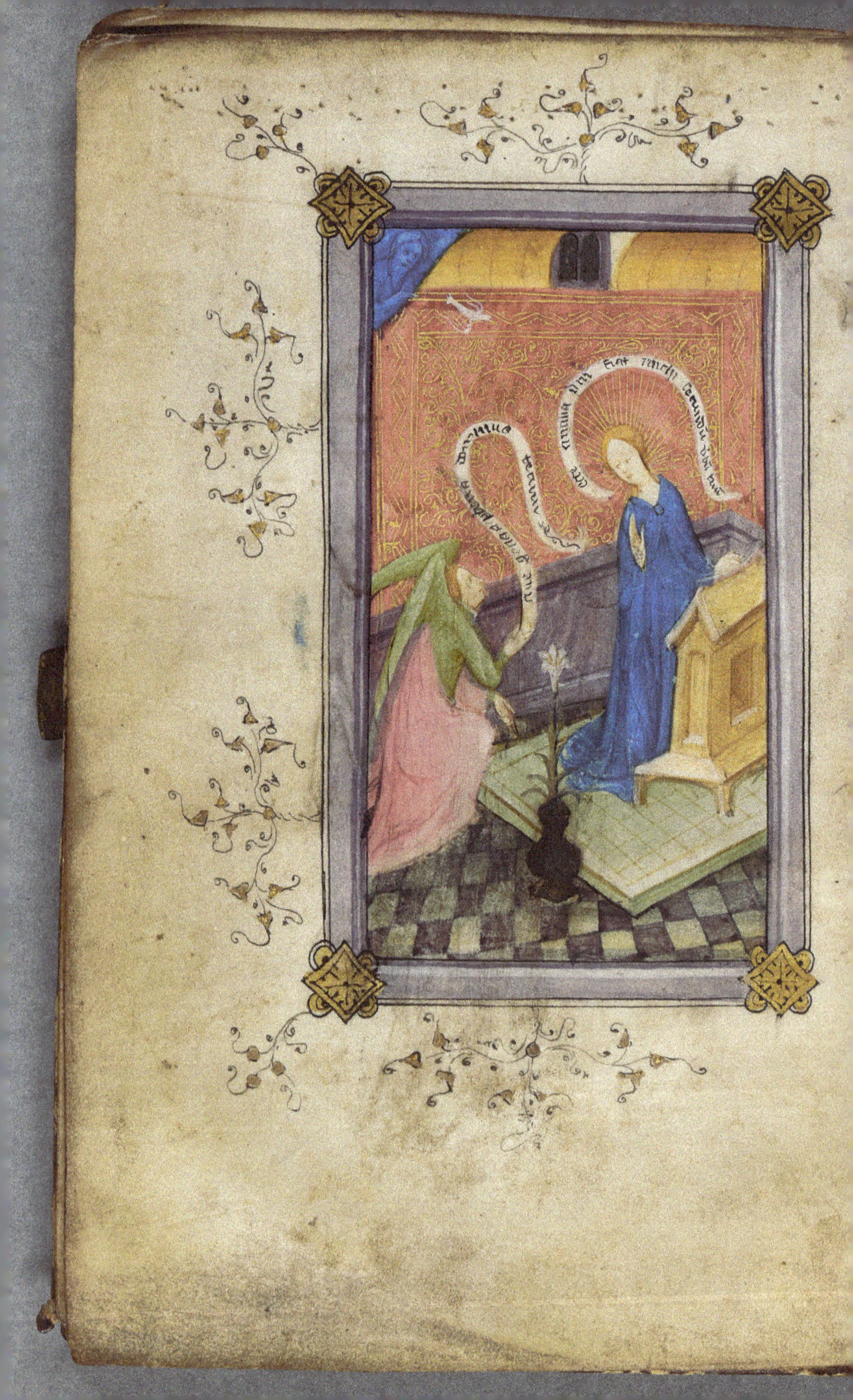

calendar, and, as just noted, he is allotted a suffrage). The English saints in the litany here are Edward, Dunstan, Sexburga and Milburga.

A distinction relating to the making of the manuscripts is that, whereas Ushaw 10 contains some miniatures done on singletons and others that were painted directly onto sheets bearing text as an integral part of the volume, all the miniatures in the present manuscript are (or rather were—many are now lost) on singletons and were evidently made separately from the main body of the book. This production-line approach, in which the southern Netherlands excelled, expedited the manufacturing process, helping to make such volumes easy to customize yet economically viable. It did not, however, guarantee accuracy: Dunstan's name was misspelled in the litany, while Becket was incorrectly described as "apostle" rather than "bishop" or "martyr" at his primary feast in the calendar.

There are also differences between the two books in terms of the choice of pigments, not least blue: whereas in Ushaw 10 lapis lazuli was invariably used, in the present manuscript the cheaper mineral azurite was preferred, albeit with some slight admixture of lapis. Equally, more extensive use was made here of economical earth colours. (The palette comprises: red—organic; pink—organic; purple—organic; orange—red lead; yellow—ochre; green—indigo in the miniatures, copper-based plus organic in the initials; blue—azurite, indigo; brown—ochre, organic; white—white lead; black—carbon; gold leaf (untooled) and gold ink.) Nevertheless, it was the miniatures of the present manuscript, not those of Ushaw 10, that were protected by fabric curtains (as sewing holes at the top of the relevant pages show).

A different sort of contrast with Ushaw 10 is that, while that book was much-augmented by its early owners, generally in English, the only additions made to the present manuscript were three short and widely current Latin prayers designated *Pro peste mutorum animalium*, *Pro mortalitate hominum* and *Pro fame et pestilencia*. These were appended by a single fifteenth-century hand to the *oraisons* following the litany (49v).

Other than the masculine forms of certain prayers, indicating that the manuscript was designed for a man, there is no evidence of medieval provenance. An inscription on 1r records that in 1696 the book belonged to a George Meynell Junior by gift of his father; this was witnessed by a "Barba: Medcalf of Barningham"; the name George Meynell is also written on 48r. The men are perhaps the Georges Meynell of Aldborough, North Yorkshire, who were both reported as "popish recusants" at the Quarter Sessions held at Thirsk in April 1716, the Barningham being that which was (until 1972) in the North Riding of Yorkshire.

23. Hours and Devotions. England; $XV^{1/2}$

Ff. i (parchment stub, unnumbered: medieval service book fragment) + 150 + viii (*s.* xvi paper, unnumbered) + i (parchment stub: medieval service book fragment). 107x72 (75x47) mm. Lines: 14. Ruling: ink. Quiring: generally 8s (occasionally imperfect), smaller at the ends of each part. Composed of five separable parts: A) fols. 1–54; B) fols. 55–75; C) fols. 76–131; D) fols. 132–146; E) fols. 147–150. Contemporary catchwords in A–D (a different style in each part). Binding, *s.* xvi^2: pasteboard covered in brown calf, outlined with blind fillets, female bust in profile within a patterned ovoid embossed in gold at the centre of both boards; 4 bands; head- and tail-band sewing in blue and white twine (discoloured); holes near the fore-edge of the boards for 2 clasps (one at the midpoint, the other towards the bottom).

Moriarty 6 (illustration: fol. 75v)

This intriguing volume comprises four main sections (A–D) plus a smaller, fragmentary, fifth and final one (E), all with the same line count, but each written by a different scribe and each with its own form of visual articulation. Books of Hours were not infrequently manufactured in self-contained sections by different scribes in order to expedite production—but usually maintaining a more homogenous appearance than here. Moreover, Parts D and E of the present volume would most naturally be dated later than Parts A and B, with Part C even later. Many *horae* were expanded with supplements to tailor them to the needs of subsequent owners. What is striking here, however, is that each of the main sections received its own additions, and that none of the augmenting hands responsible for these early supplements appears in more than one Part. This favours the view that each Part initially had an independent existence. The volume might therefore have been built up over a generation or more during the first half of the fifteenth century, with the early assemblage of Parts A and B being subsequently augmented with Parts D, E and finally C. Alternatively, it could represent a single act of compilation or salvage—undertaken at any point between the writing of Part C and the provision of the current

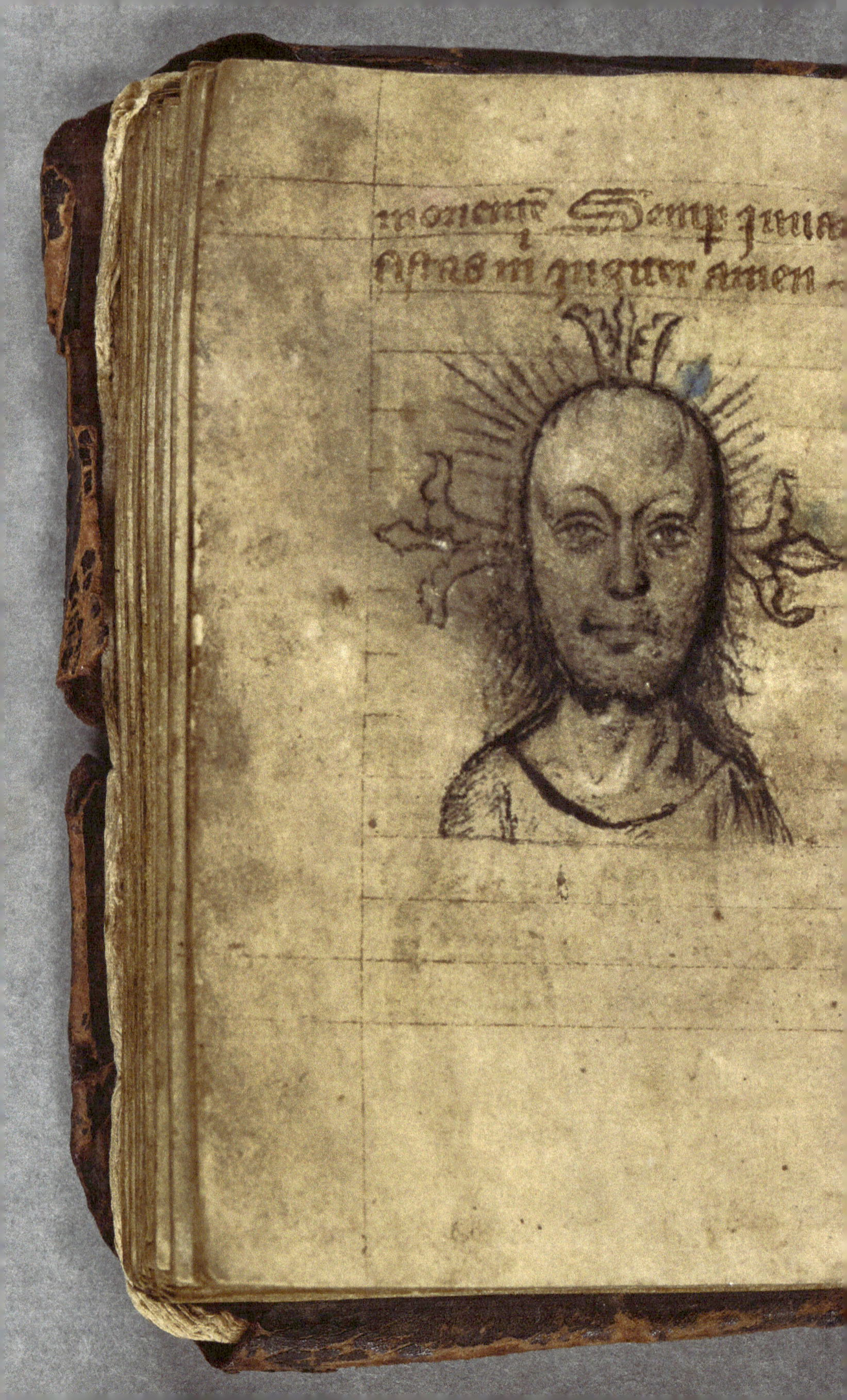

binding during the second half of the sixteenth century—in which parts from originally separate *horae* or prayerbooks with the same line count were brought together. The fact that the volume starts with the Hours of the Trinity (not a calendar or the Hours of the Virgin) and lacks a set of suffrages favours this interpretation. The manuscript is thus potentially an example of the creative recycling of texts for private devotion and is interesting as such, irrespective of whether this was undertaken in the fifteenth century or the sixteenth, before or after the Reformation.

The core of Part A is the Hours of the Trinity followed by devotions to the cross, and a suffrage for St Margaret; that of Part B is an acephalous Hours for Sapientia; of Part C, the Psalter of Jerome, formulae for confession, the penitential psalms, litany and prayers; of Part D the litany of the Virgin plus Marian prayers; the small and lacunose Part E has further prayers—to Christ (for a male suppliant) and to God the Father (now imperfect)—plus a now-incomplete Marian devotion. Part A was augmented with supplementary texts for Margaret (52v, line 11–54v), Part B with a prayer to a guardian angel (75r–v, male suppliant) and an image of the Holy Face of Christ (75v), Part C with "Stabat mater" (130r–131v), D with a suffrage for Mary Magdalene (146v).

The volume includes one rubric in French and one in English. The former (76r, "Ici comence le sautier seint Jerome le prestre") heads the Psalter of Jerome at the start of Part C. The latter (47v–48r) follows the devotion to the cross near the end of Part A. In fact, the devotion in question ("O crux salve preciosa, O crux salve gloriosa . . . ") is specifically associated in other manuscripts with the Rood of Bromholm (a supposed relic of the True Cross acquired by Bro[o]mholm priory, Norfolk, in the early thirteenth century), and this is the case here too. For the rubric reads: "Thys cros þat here peyntyd is, signe of þe cros of bromholm is, þat cros is made of pecis fine þat cryst on bledde in hese pine [i.e. pain]. Iesus nazarenus rex iudeorum". The image in question, now missing, was (staining shows) made separately and pasted into a space (60x50 mm) left vacant for it: it was probably one of the devotional cards showing the Rood that were produced for distribution to pilgrims and of which an example survives, stuck into a book of hours in Lambeth Palace Library (MS 545).

It is this rood that the miller's wife invokes in Chaucer's "The Reeve's Tale" when, having unwittingly slept with one clerk, she is suddenly awoken by her husband who, brawling with the other clerk, falls on to her: "And with the fal out of hir sleep she breyde | Help hooly croys of Bromeholm she seyde" (ll. 4285–6). (Staining suggests that a second image may formerly have been pasted to fol. 54v of our book; if so, it presumably portrayed St Margaret.)

The most elaborately ornamented "original" pages appear at the start of Parts A and C, the former distinguished by a decorated initial plus all-round border (1r), the latter by a golden capital with border bar and sprays (76r). The pigments used on 1r are red—vermilion, organic, vermilion plus organic; orange—red lead, red lead plus organic; blue—azurite; white—white lead; along with gold leaf over gesso. Those on 76r are: red—vermilion; green—copper; blue—azurite; purple—organic; plus gold leaf. The image that was added to fol. 75v (the end of part B) depicts the face of Christ and was probably done (its style suggests) around 1500 or in the early sixteenth century. Drawn in carbon black, with the eyes and chin discreetly highlighted in white lead, it is a version of a type of Holy Face, popular in the Low Countries during the fifteenth century, that reflects archetypes painted in 1438 and 1440 by Jan van Eyck which are now only known from early copies.

The circumstance that the only saints afforded a suffrage are Margaret and Mary Magdalene might seem to point to female use; however, the prayers with gender-specific words have male forms (" . . . me tibi commissum salva . . . ", fol. 75r; " . . . me miserum peccatorem N famulum tuum . . . ", fol. 148v) without the female alternatives even inserted. Moreover, the uncertain status of the volume as it has come down to us—whether it represents a curated, as opposed to an opportunistic, assemblage—adds to the difficulties of profiling its first user(s) from its current contents. The earliest evidence of provenance is an inscription added to one of the paper endleaves in a *s.* xvi–xvii Italic: "hic | Harry parry / est Liber / meus" ("Harry" is repeated by the same hand on another page).

24. Psalter and Manual (The "Bobbingworth Psalter"). Southern England; XIV/XV

Ff. iv (*s*. xviii paper) + 184 + iv (*s*. xviii paper). 356x240 (256x171) mm. 2 cols.; 24 lines. Ruling: ink (violet). Quiring: 8s. Contemporary catchwords. Binding, *s*. xviii: millboard covered in red-brown leather, tooled with a panel plus corner fleurons; 6 narrow bands, the spine zones tooled with foliate patterns; the edges of the book-block gilded and goffered.

Ushaw 8 (illustration: fol. 7r)

In this handsome volume, a calendar, psalter, canticles and litany (fols. 1–100) are followed by noted mass texts then orders of service for baptism, marriage (134r–143r), visiting the sick, absolution, the dead (vigil and mass, commendation of souls, burial service), ending with Gregory's "trental" (requiem masses) and the start of John's Gospel (1.1–14). The only English saints named in the litanies on 98r–v and 126r–v are Alban, Swithun, Birinus and Edith, to whom are added Edmund, Æthelwold, Dunstan and Cuthbert in that on 149r–v. In the *ordo* for baptism (122r–134r), feminine forms were supplied interlinearly in red.

The writing of the main body of the book was shared between two scribes (responsible for eleven and twelve quires respectively, the changeover occurring in the middle of the *Te deum*, fols. 94v/95r); both used Textualis semi-quadrata, the hand of the first more elongated and less angular than that of the second. The calendar was penned in a smaller, slightly more compressed version of the second style. The principal textual divisions within the book are marked by decorated initials plus full borders; a lost page preceding the canon of the mass doubtless bore an image of the crucifixion. Each new text is headed by an enlarged initial in gold leaf set against panels of blue and burgundy; verses within the psalter are headed by gold then blue initials in alternation, flourished in dark blue/purple and red respectively. The pigments are red—vermilion; orange—red lead; pink—vermilion plus organic; green—copper-based; blue—azurite in the major decoration, lapis lazuli for minor initials and line-fillers;

white—white lead; and gold leaf (untooled). In addition, an organic yellow was used to highlight calligraphic capitals, above all those heading sections of chant. The black ink is gallo-tannic. An interesting feature here is the consistent, counter-intuitive use of the more expensive lapis blue for minor initials, and the cheaper azurite in the major decoration.

The texts are entirely in Latin except for the vows within the wedding service, which are given in English (fol. 134r; cf. **no. 19**): "I N take þe N in to my weddid wyfe to haue and to holde for þis day forward, for better, for wers for richer, for porer, in sekeness and in hele, til deth us departe, gif holy chirche hit wol ordeyne, and þerto I pligt þe my trewþe"; "I N take þe N in to my weddid housebonde to haue and to holde fro þis day foreward for better for wers, for richer for porer, in sekenesse and in helle to be boner and buxum in bedde and borde til deth us departe, gif holy chirche hit wol ordeyne, and þerto I pligt þe my treuthe."

Family records added to the calendar by several hands, plus the inserted dedication feast of the church at High Ongar (*alta honger*, 20 June), link the book to the Walsinghams of Scadbury, Kent, who held the manor of Bobbingworth, the parish adjacent to High Ongar, Essex. Other people commemorated are William Estfeld/Eastfield, Mayor of London (d. 1446; fol. 3r), and Henry Beaufort, named only via his title "Lord Cardinal Bishop of Winchester" (d. 1447; fol. 2v), both of whom were connected to the Walsinghams via Thomas Walsingham (d. 1457—his death duly recorded on 3v), a prosperous London vintner-entrepreneur who supplied wine to Beaufort's household. It was Thomas who purchased Scadbury (1424). All these records, which extend in date from 1416 (1v) to 1485 (5v), are in Latin.

A final entry was made in or shortly after 1550, this time in English: "Sir Edmund Walsyngham dyed the 9 of thys month [February; 1v] in the [?thry]d of Edward vj". By this time, the book had been modestly adapted to Protestant requirements via the erasure of all "pape"s from the calendar and the crossing through of the first page of the mass texts and the second page of the second litany (mainly saints as opposed to apostles); however, the corresponding page of the first litany was untouched, as were all three feasts of Thomas Becket in the calendar.

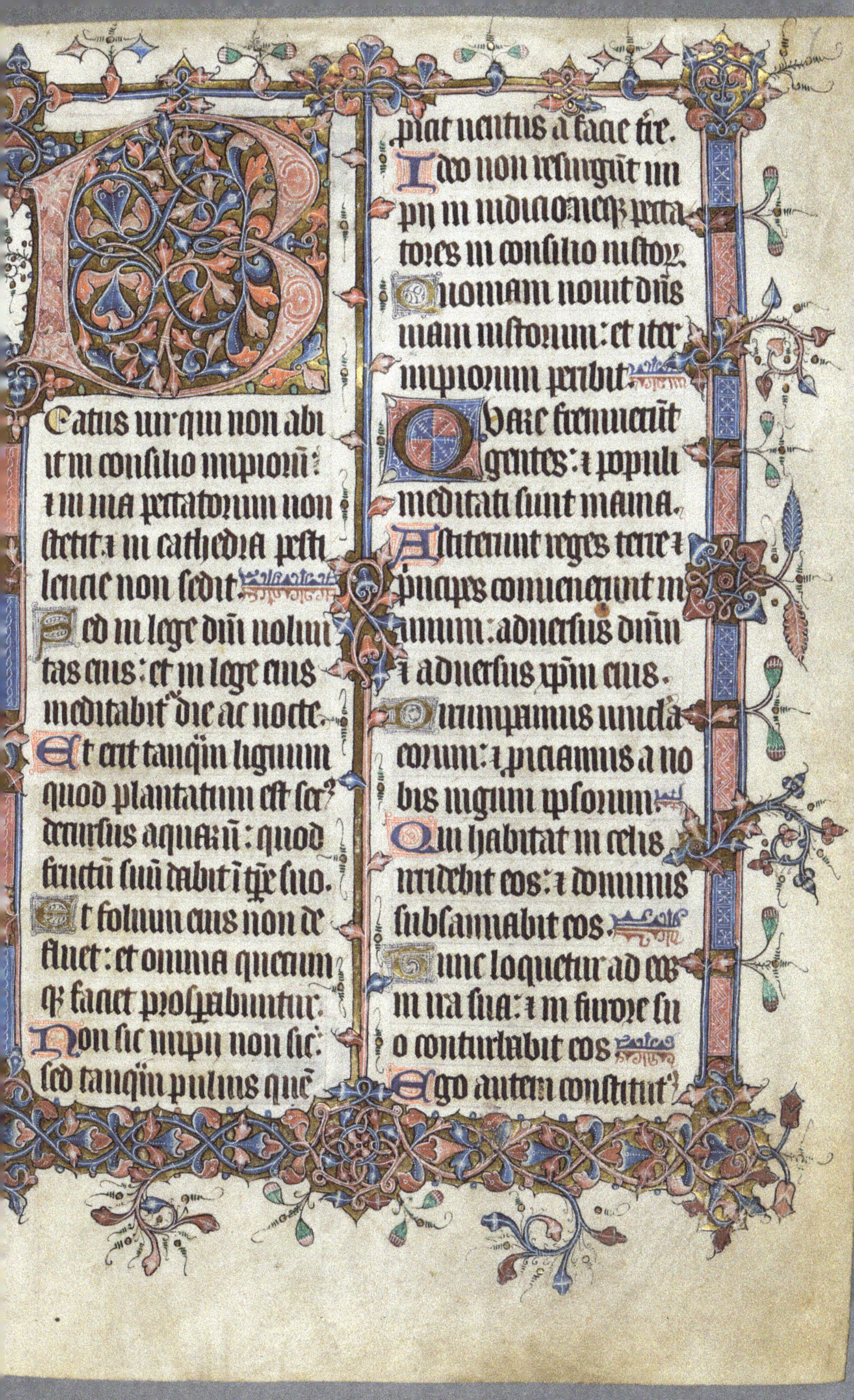

Beatus uir qui non abi
it in consilio impiorum:
& in uia peccatorum non
stetit: & in cathedra pesti
lencie non sedit.
Sed in lege domini uolun
tas eius: et in lege eius
meditabitur die ac nocte.
Et erit tanquam lignum
quod plantatum est secus
decursus aquarum: quod
fructum suum dabit in tempore suo.
Et folium eius non de
fluet: et omnia quecum
que faciet prosperabuntur.
Non sic impii non sic:
sed tanquam puluis quem
proicit uentus a facie terre.
Ideo non resurgunt im
pii in iudicio: neque pecca
tores in consilio iustorum.
Quoniam nouit dominus
uiam iustorum: et iter
impiorum peribit.
Quare fremuerunt
gentes: & populi
meditati sunt inania.
Astiterunt reges terre &
principes conuenerunt in
unum: aduersus dominum
& aduersus christum eius.
Dirumpamus uincula
eorum: & proiciamus a no
bis iugum ipsorum.
Qui habitat in celis
irridebit eos: & dominus
subsannabit eos.
Tunc loquetur ad eos
in ira sua: & in furore su
o conturbabit eos.
Ego autem constitutus

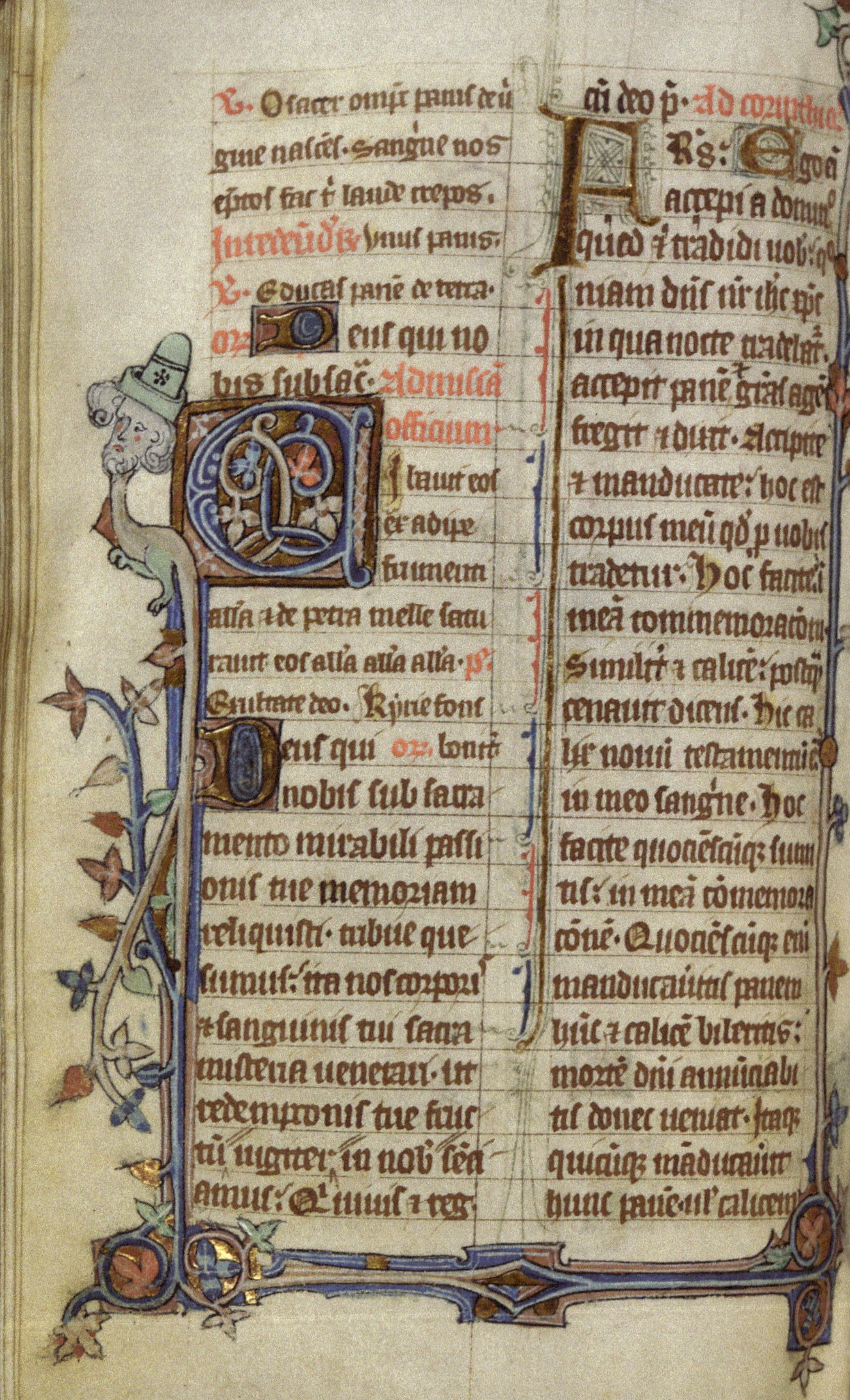

℣. O sacer omnium panis de ui-
gine nascens. Sangue nos
emnos fac tibi laude repos.
Inter[illegible] Unus panis.
℣. Educas panem de terra.
Or. Deus qui no-
bis sub sac. Ad missam
officium.
Cibauit eos
ex adipe
frumenti
alleluia et de petra melle satu-
rauit eos alleluia alleluia alleluia. Ps.
Exultate deo. Kyrie fons.
Deus qui Or. Bonitas
nobis sub sacra-
mento mirabili passi-
onis tue memoriam
reliquisti. tribue que-
sumus: ita nos corporis
et sanguinis tui sacra
misteria uenerari. ut
redemptionis tue fruc-
tum iugiter: in nobis senti-
amus: Qui uiuis et reg-
nas cum deo patre. Ad corinthios.
Rs: Ego enim
accepi a domino
quod et tradidi uobis: quoniam dominus noster ihesus christus
in qua nocte tradebatur.
accepit panem gratias agens
fregit et dixit. Accipite
et manducate: hoc est
corpus meum quod pro uobis
tradetur. Hoc facite in
meam commemorationem.
Simul et calicem: postquam
cenauit dicens. Hic ca-
lix noui testamenti est
in meo sanguine. Hoc
facite quotienscumque sumi-
tis: in meam commemora-
tionem. Quotienscumque enim
manducabitis panem
hunc et calicem bibetis:
mortem domini annunciabi-
tis donec ueniat. Itaque
quicumque manducauerit
hunc panem uel calicem

25. Missal (Sarum; creed and common prefaces noted) (The "Goldwell Missal"). Southern England; XIV[1]

Ff. 502. 191x130 (146x84) mm. 2 columns, 25 lines. Ruling: ink. Quiring: mainly 8s and 6s. Contemporary catchwords; the major supplements have catchwords, quire letters and leaf numbers. Binding, *s.* xvii (rebacked): pasteboard covered in vellum (with older parchment pastedowns), double fillet gold border and central panel with corner fleurons; 6 bands; head- and tail-band sewing blue and yellow. Stains on the first and last leaves from the metal fixtures of a single strap-and-pin fastening on an earlier binding.

Ushaw 18 (illustration: fol. 260v)

Corrections, additions, substitutions, multiple supplements (the most substantial being four quires of Sequences, fols. 465–96) and a reordering, almost all neatly done, attest to extensive use and customization of the volume, starting at an early date and continuing well into the fifteenth century. The calendar, by contrast, was little altered, with only four feasts being added to it—the Visitation, the Translation of St Hugh, and the Deposition and Translation of St Osmund. As Osmund was only canonized in 1457, he appears as an insertion in many service books; however, the fact that not only were both of his feasts added to the calendar but, in addition, the texts for a votive mass specified for use on either occasion were appended to the volume (fol. 499r) points to a closer association with Salisbury. Such would accord with the circumstance that the earliest recorded owner of the book, James Goldwell, was a prebendary of Salisbury from 1462, becoming its dean the following year.

An informally written Latin inscription on 2v states, "Estwell by gift of the Reverend Father and Lord James Goldwell formerly bishop of Norwich AD 1504". Goldwell was elevated to the see of Norwich in 1472, holding it until his death in 1499. The explanation for his bequest of the book to Eastwell, near Ashford in Kent, is presumably that it was close to his family manor of Great Chart (of whose own parish church he was a great patron). Many of the varied benefactions to diverse individuals and institutions recorded in Goldwell's will (which included other service books and legal texts) were explicitly made in return for prayers for his soul: there was doubtless an assumption that the same would result from the present volume. The prayer specified in the original stratum of the manuscript itself for use in masses for dead benefactors (451v) reads: "Miserere quesumus domine animabus omnium benefactorum nostrorum defunctorum et pro beneficiis que nobis largiti sunt in terris, premia eterna consequantur in celis" ("Have mercy, O Lord we beseech you, on the souls of all our deceased benefactors; and for the gifts that they lavished on us in the world, may they obtain eternal rewards in heaven."). In addition, one of six votive masses appended to the book was a common service for parents and benefactors (497v–498r): what was sought here was, similarly, that God would remit their sins and grant them eternal life.

The main divisions within the original text are marked by decorated initials plus border bars. The ornamentation of the initials is restricted to foliate scrolls and interlocking tubes plus, on one occasion (48r), a mask. A few of the bars feature a single motif such as a dragon (19r) or a hybrid (260v, 310r) along with the ubiquitous foliate forms; that at the canon of the mass (206r) incorporates a human figure, possibly haloed, hands apparently clasped in prayer, who looks towards the preceding page (now lost) on which will doubtless have been an image of the crucifixion. The style of the artwork has been likened to that of a psalter made for Christ Church, Canterbury (Bodleian Library, Auct. D.2.2), and also to the initials in the De Lisle Psalter (British Library, Arundel 83 (part II)). Subdivisions are headed by golden initials, alternately flourished in red and blue and/or violet, then set against pink and blue panels; those in the main supplement have green and gold sprays sprouting from their letter panels. The pigments are: red—vermilion; orange—red lead; pink—organic, vermilion plus organic; green—copper-based; blue—azurite; black—carbon; white—lead; and gold leaf (sometimes applied over a ground tinted with red lead).

26. Missal (Sarum, noted). England; XIV^{med}

Ff. i (modern paper) + 2 (medieval flyleaves) + 257 + 2 (medieval flyleaves) + i (modern paper). Two modern foliations, one starting with the first flyleaf, the other with the first leaf of the main book and omitting "65". 382x256 (286x183) mm. 2 columns; 35 lines. Ruling: red ink. Quiring: 12s. Contemporary catchwords; quire letter plus leaf number in the first half of quires. Numerous parchment tabs stuck or sewn to, or laced into, leaves. Binding, *s.* xx: bevelled wooden boards covered in leather; 5 bands. Stains on former pastedowns indicate an earlier binding with seven sewing stations, the board channels at right angles to the spine; metal fixtures.

Moriarty 5 (illustration: fol. 7r)

This functional yet imposing missal has seen heavy use, as the weathering of its leaves and the extreme darkening of the pages bearing the common prefaces attest. The most substantial supplement, mass texts for St Anne (fol. 258 [259] r–v), was doubtless a response to the promotion of her feast for celebration in England by Pope Urban VI in 1383. The major textual divisions are headed by decorated initials plus border bars, adorned with spiky leaves and other foliate forms, eye-catching but crudely done. All other subdivisions are marked by blue initials of different sizes, flourished in red. The pigments used were: red (for flourishing and rubric)—vermilion; pink—organic; orange—red lead; green—copper-based, plus indigo; blue—azurite; white—white lead. The ink is gallo-tannic.

The inclusion in the *sanctorale* (181v) of an original entry for Chad with a rubric declaring: "Sancti Cedde non de usu sarum, sed de usu lichifeldensis diocesis" (" . . . not according to the use of Sarum but according to the use of Lichfield Diocese") points to a connection with the Diocese of Lichfield-Coventry. A fifteenth-century hand amplified the provision, adding in the margin Luke 12:32 as an alternative Gospel reading should the feast (2 March) fall in Lent, and providing a cross-reference to the Translation of St Martin (194r–v), where the reading was already given in full.

A preponderance of the obits added to the calendar are for members of the Scriven (Screuen/Scryven/Screwyn) family of Frodesley (Fradisleye), Shropshire, the earliest being Elizabeth, who died in 1416, the latest being Thomas, who died in 1533; correspondingly, "Dedicatio ecclesie de Fradisleye" was inserted *in rasura* on 11 January. The key figure for this phase in the history of the volume was surely the John Scriven who was recorded as an assessor at Shrewsbury in 1392–3 and 1400–1, then bailiff there in 1402–3 and 1406–7, since it was he who acquired (by marriage) the manor of Frodesley. The Reginald Scriven to whom the benefice was awarded in 1406 was doubtless a relative, and it was under his aegis, presumably, that family obits started to be inserted a decade later.

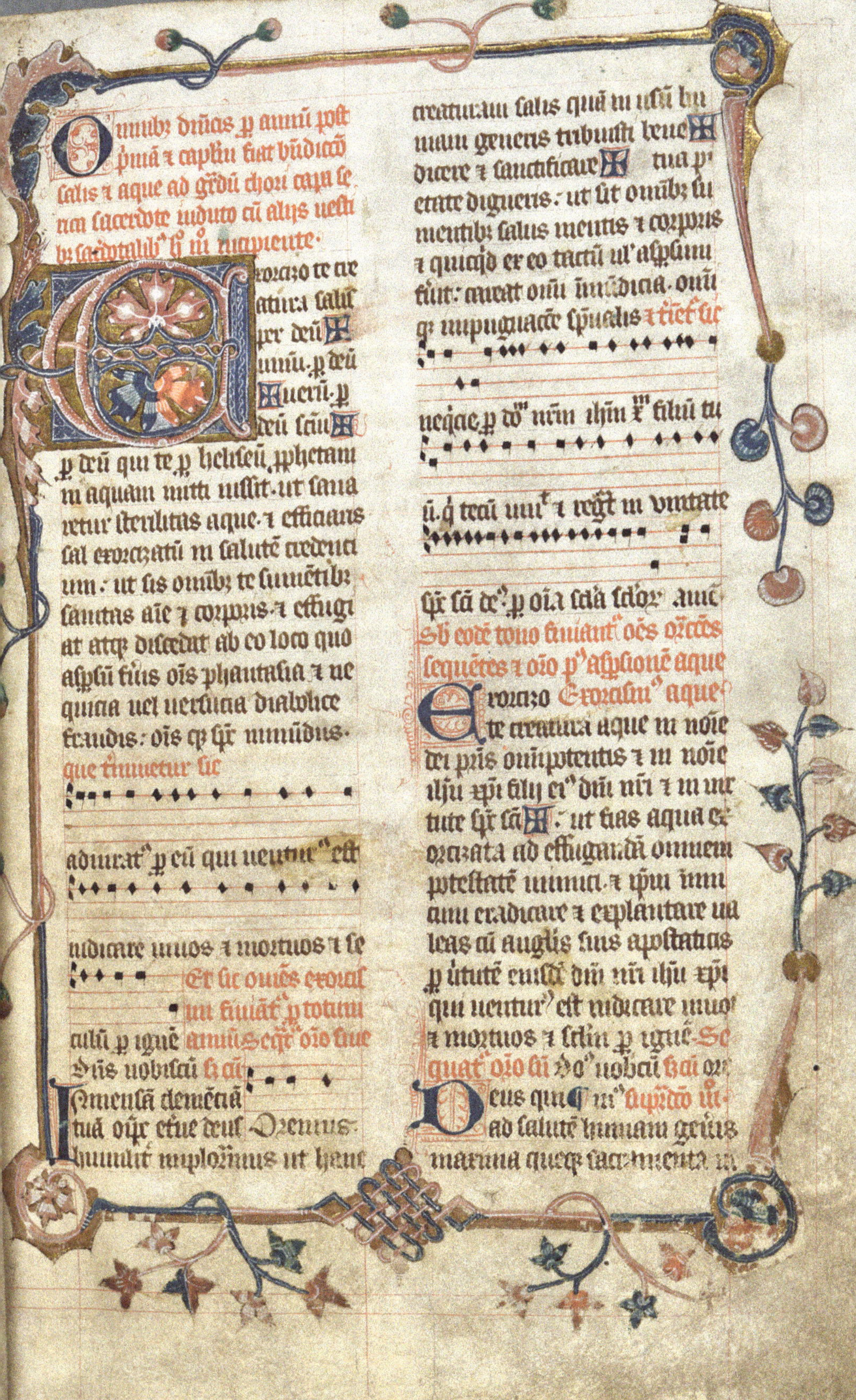

Omnibus dominicis per annum post primam et capitulum fiat benedictio salis et aque ad gradum chori a sacerdote induto cum aliis vestibus sacerdotalibus sic incipiente.

Exorcizo te creatura salis per deum + vivum, per deum + verum, per deum sanctum + per deum qui te per heliseum prophetam in aquam mitti iussit ut sanaretur sterilitas aque. et efficiaris sal exorcizatum in salutem credentium: ut sis omnibus te sumentibus sanitas anime et corporis. et effugiat atque discedat ab eo loco quo aspersum fueris omnis phantasia et nequicia vel versucia diabolice fraudis: omnisque spiritus immundus. que finietur sic

adiuratus per eum qui venturus est

iudicare vivos et mortuos et seculum per ignem. Et sic omnes exorcismi finiantur per totum annum. Sequatur oratio sine Dominus vobiscum sic dicendo. Oremus.

Immensam clementiam tuam omnipotens eterne deus humiliter imploramus ut hanc creaturam salis quam in usum humani generis tribuisti bene+dicere et sancti+ficare tua pietate digneris: ut sit omnibus sumentibus salus mentis et corporis et quicquid ex eo tactum vel aspersum fuerit: careat omni immundicia. omnique impugnacione spiritualis nequicie. Per dominum nostrum ihesum christum filium tuum

qui tecum vivit et regnat in unitate

spiritus sancti deus. Per omnia secula seculorum. Amen.

Sub eodem tono finiantur omnes orationes sequentes et oratio post aspersionem aque. Exorcismus aque.

Exorcizo te creatura aque in nomine dei patris omnipotentis et in nomine ihesu christi filii eius domini nostri et in virtute spiritus sancti +. ut fias aqua exorcizata ad effugandam omnem potestatem inimici. et ipsum inimicum eradicare et explantare valeas cum angelis suis apostatis per virtutem eiusdem domini nostri ihesu christi qui venturus est iudicare vivos et mortuos et seculum per ignem. Sequatur oratio sine Dominus vobiscum.

Deus qui ad salutem humani generis maxima quecumque sacramenta in

Concordance

Index

References are to catalogue numbers, except when the numeral is preceded by an 'I', in which case it refers to a page number of the Introduction. Medieval personages are indexed under their first name, post-medieval people under their surname.

EU GPSR Authorized Representative:

LOGOS EUROPE, 9 rue Nicolas Poussin, 17000 La Rochelle, France

contact@logoseurope.eu

www.ingramcontent.com/pod-product-compliance
Lightning Source LLC
LaVergne TN
LVHW052347100826
845147LV00012B/777

* 9 7 8 1 7 8 9 5 9 1 8 5 9 *